SOUL CONSCIOUSNESS

Embrace the Journey Within

SHREYASI SHUKLA

"To my past: Through adversity's forge, you awakened my true inner strength. Grateful for your journey; you illuminate my path forward".

CONTENTS

Welcome Note

It is with heartfelt joy and immense gratitude that we extend our warmest welcome to the fantastic realm of "Soul Consciousness." This magnificent book is more than just a piece of literature; it is a journey into the depths of the human psyche, an investigation of the infinite potential of the human spirit, and a discovery of the fundamental oneness of all life.

We live in a fast-paced, materialistic society where it is easy to become caught up in the tornado of daily routines, become preoccupied with the external chase of success, and become overwhelmed by the noise of modern life. The concept of "soul consciousness" encourages us to step back, contemplate our lives, and investigate the timeless truths endured throughout the ages. It enables us to think about something beyond the mundane: the possibility that we are immortal souls, inextricably tied to the heavenly source that sustains all existence.

The Soul Consciousness Quest

This is more than just a collection of words; it explores who we are. It compels us to pierce the veil of everyday life and investigate the core of who we are as human beings. It prompts us to ponder one of life's most fundamental inquiries: Who are we?

As you will learn in these pages, the key is to acknowledge our divine bond. It's a recognition of how every one of us is an essential part of the more extraordinary fabric of the universe. We are not distinct from the divine; we are an integral part of it.

The Force of Ideas and Deeds

However, "Soul Consciousness" is more than just a philosophical treatise; it's also a how-to manual for tapping into the vast potential of our minds and bodies. It serves as a timely reminder that the ripple effects of our decisions, actions, and motivations can be felt for generations.

As you absorb the knowledge presented here, you'll see that your existence isn't just a collection of random events but rather the result of a complex web of causes and consequences. Your decisions and actions have far-reaching consequences that affect not only your life but also the world at large.

Reincarnation and the Law of Karma

It reveals the hidden meanings behind these time-tested concepts. "Soul Consciousness" acts as your guide to interpreting the threads of cause and effect that weave the intricate pattern of your existence.

You can learn more about the continuity of life and the opportunities for spiritual development throughout many incarnations by investigating karma and reincarnation. This insight can serve as a map that helps you make decisions that align with your highest values.

A Shining Example for Today's World

"Soul consciousness" provides comfort and insight into a world that sometimes feels tumultuous and unclear. It serves as a timely reminder that despite the external turmoil, each of us has the power to cultivate tranquillity within, to shine a light for others, and to make a difference in not only our own lives but the lives of those around us.

This book equips you to live a life of purpose, compassion, and heightened awareness as you negotiate the complex web of your thoughts, actions, and intentions. It's a guide to living with purpose, making decisions out of love, and using every day as a chance to grow spiritually.

A Quest for Identity

May the eternal wisdom that fills the pages of "Soul Consciousness" serve as a motivation for you as you embark on this profound journey of self-discovery. This knowledge, from many different spiritual traditions, goes beyond dogma to highlight the oneness at the heart of all difference.

Please ponder the lessons and absorb the timeless truths that have inspired seekers of knowledge throughout the years. This book has something to teach everyone, whether they are serious about their spiritual development or just interested in exploring the meaning of life. It's a wealth of information and insight that can help you better comprehend the universe and your place in it.

An Experience That Will Change Your Life

This book is not only a compilation of words; it is a profound investigation of the essence of our existence. It encourages you to come to terms with your divinity, to learn the value of soul consciousness, and to find your way through the complexities of karma and rebirth.

With profound appreciation, we extend the invitation to enter a realm of awakening and renewal. May your soul's potential be unlocked, your consciousness raised, and your life filled with meaning and purpose as you read these words.

Embark on a journey of self-discovery with "Soul Consciousness." I am overjoyed to have you along for this life-altering trip.

Introduction

Welcome to "Soul Consciousness," a trip into the deep spiritual realms. This is not your average spiritual quest; rather, it's an ode to the insatiable curiosity of the human spirit and the common questions that unite us all.

The age-old query "Who am I?" is where the adventure starts. To comprehend the connection that binds us all together, this inquiry probes profoundly into the nature of who we are.

Below the surface of life, we find our aura, a dynamic field of energy that reflects our feelings and overall state of being. This subtle atmosphere, which is sometimes disregarded, reveals a lot about our inner selves.

The path of life has resulted in the complex network of karma, which is a universe in which deeds and their repercussions are not limited by time or location. Our quest for self-discovery has been greatly aided by our comprehension of karma and its consequences.

Through the investigation of soul connections, we see the mysterious ties that bind soulmates and kindred spirits together, surpassing the limits of logic and reason. These links serve as a reminder of our common human experience and can defy explanation.

In the face of obstacles and misfortunes in life, we have discovered the transforming potential of self-love—a journey that goes beyond simple acceptance of oneself to include accepting flaws and appreciating the deep beauty that lies inside.

Life is full of change, which we have learnt to welcome with open arms. Our capacity to deal with life's obstacles with grace and resilience has been influenced by our path of knowing the ebb and flow of life's changes.

We have found that the present moment has the transforming potential, even in a culture that frequently encourages moping over the past or fretting over the future. It is a gift of great delight and tranquillity.

We set out on this journey of self-discovery and enlightenment together. Anticipate delving into the core of your feelings, experiencing epiphanies, and discovering the light at the end of your own road. This is not a unique voyage; rather, it is an invitation to ponder life's big issues, the wonder of our interconnected souls, and the metamorphosis that results from accepting change, loving oneself, and living in the now. Come along with us on this journey of self-discovery and spiritual development.

We are going to go deep into my feelings as we go through the pages of "Soul Consciousness," and hope that these insights will help to discover new sense of self identity. This is not simply my journey; it is an invitation to delve into the deepest mysteries of life, the wonder of our interconnected souls, and the transformation found in self-acceptance, self-improvement, and present-moment living. Let us go out on this journey of love, enlightenment, and self-discovery together.

With this book, I invite you to lift up from body consciousness which opens up your unlimited potential for personal power as well as Spiritual transformation.

CHAPTER 1

Who am I?

The question "Who am I?" has captivated researchers, scientists, and intellectuals from various fields throughout human knowledge. Despite the wealth of human knowledge, it is a question that has yet to escape straightforward answers from the empirical world of science to the nuances of human behaviour in psychology and through the corridors of history and culture.

In science, we have discovered the fundamental building blocks of our physical existence—atoms and subatomic particles. However, this astonishing insight into the mechanics of our physical body does not reveal the heart of our conscious Self, the "I" that ponders and experiences the universe. There have been many attempts in ancient times, found in various subjects, to find the answer to the question. For example, in psychology, the study of human behaviour and emotions delves deeply into the complexity of the human mind. However, it confronts a dilemma. The illusive "self," at the heart of psychological investigation, is an abstract term difficult to explain concretely.

History reveals the stories of human civilization, reflecting cultural and societal constructions. Subjective opinions create it, and the "self" it portrays is a multidimensional construct shaped by cultural conventions.

Philosophy has provided several viewpoints on the nature of the Self through intense thought and intellectual rigor. A definitive response to the question remains to be discovered. We can get insights into the intangible components of human experience in art, literature, and creative expression. They provide light on our inner world, yet the definitive answer remains to be seen, concealed by all the interpretations and perspectives that art includes. No field, perspective, or technique has answered "Who am I?" It remains a profound and persistent mystery, inviting us to pursue our journey for self-discovery and enlightenment.

The age-old question of "Who am I?" has a timeless interest in the wide span of human existence. It results from the delicate interplay between our essence as souls and the plethora of exterior identities imposed on us. We find ourselves in a society where names, roles, and cultural expectations can conceal the profound core of our inner selves. There have been many attempts to find the answer to this question in various fields like religion, science, metaphysics, philosophy, etc. At the same time, there have been some attempts to suppress this question due to the overwhelming burden that it carries.

In the human mind, which is eager to know about what happens to us after death, what is real? But as long as death is there, these suppressions will be unsuccessful. We may talk with others about seeing nothing and believing nothing beyond our senses. We may limit our sense of experience to the present moment only. We might restrict ourselves in this 3-dimensional world and see nothing beyond this physical body. The consciousness of the whole world is shallow, which does not add anything to our superconscious state. Yet, if death is there, these questions will come up again and again. Is death the end of all things to which we cling? Is nothing real and permanent? The world vanishes in a moment, and everything is gone. Everyone is at some point bound to ask, Is this real? The dreams and aspirations of lifetimes build up and are gone in a split second. Is this real?

Our journey begins at birth when we are forced into a world that is eager to label and categorize us. It starts with the names our parents give us and progresses to labels like "boy" or "girl," prospective professions, and more, all aimed at providing a sense of context and belonging. However, as these labels accumulate, they may both promote and limit us, directing us down a set path while restricting our understanding of ourselves and realizing our natural sense of Self. With the greatest of intentions, parents are frequently the first to label their children.

These labels cover everything from gender stereotypes to future goals. While they provide a basis and a sense of direction, they can also influence our self-concept in ways inconsistent with our genuine nature. Parents' hopes and aspirations may unintentionally shape who we become, frequently at the expense of individual self-discovery. Society, with its rules, standards, and expectations, exerts a powerful effect outside of the family world. It determines what is normal or successful, and we, in turn, navigate a complicated web of cultural assumptions that govern our behaviour, choices, and self-worth. We must consider how these outward identities, created by cultural values, affect our view of ourselves and our role in the world.

Gender is one of the most widespread categories, influencing not only how we view ourselves but also how we interact with others and the world at large. Identifying as a "boy" or "girl" frequently influences our duties, objectives, and behaviours.

Furthermore, our achievements and accomplishments might become essential parts of our identity. The pursuit of achievement, whether academic, professional, or personal, can cause us to define ourselves through the lens of external validation. In our constant yearning for public recognition and approval, we may unwittingly conceal our true identity.

Are we primarily defined by our bodies, our minds, or even our brains? When we say "my hands," "my legs," or "my face," whose "my" are we referring to?

When pondering our identity, we frequently begin by enumerating our name, age, occupation, and other acquired characteristics. But are these labels genuinely representative of who we are, or are they life's gifts? Names, ages, occupations, and nationalities are all characteristics that we acquire throughout our lives, but our true selves lie beyond these external markers. We are given a name and taught that we are our bodies at birth. We acquire numerous titles, degrees, professions, and national affiliations as we mature. Our introduction now incorporates these developed features. For instance, a child with no notable accomplishments may become a class monitor, boosting their ego. This change occurs due to their perception of themselves as unique and superior to their counterparts. This child's ego continues to grow as they proceed through life, perhaps becoming manager, senior manager, president, and eventually CEO. They now identify themselves as the chief executive officer and demand respect commensurate with this position. Their position defines their identity.

Consequently, they expect others to revere their CEO status throughout their lives. Consider a situation in which a servant passes by without greeting him. In this instance, the CEO's ego is wounded because they perceive this as against their chosen identity. They may respond with fury, believing their position, which has become an integral part of their identity, has been demeaned.

In essence, our identity is frequently intertwined with the titles and responsibilities we acquire throughout our lives. Underneath these external trappings, however, lies a fundamental question: who are we when we remove these labels and roles? This exploration of our true essence lies at the core of the age-old query, "Who am I?"

Throughout our lives, we develop an identity based on the items we acquire and how we're taught to view ourselves.

This process is not inherent; we acquire it through our environment as we mature. When a baby is born, it does not know whether it is a male or a girl; all it feels is pure bliss. However, as the child matures, usually within a year or two, the parents often become the first to designate the child, beginning with their gender. This attachment to the body serves as the foundation for body consciousness. Then, children are taught how to conform to societal expectations, such as how to speak, act, and conduct according to their gender. When children fail to fulfill these standards, parents may respond negatively by scolding them and making them feel unworthy. This early sense of unworthiness can lead to psychological problems such as anxiety and depression later in life. When children conform to expectations, however, they receive praise, which makes them feel valid and worthy. If I am accepted, I am worthy. If I am worthy, I am loved; if I am loved, I matter; if I count, I exist.

As they grow up, they start to collect experiences and are taught to care more about what they've achieved in life. They shift from giving love and innocence to others to wanting respect and recognition for the labels they have given to themselves. This change means they lose their innocence and turn more into body consciousness.

Between 0 and 7, our brains operate in a theta brainwave state, akin to a sponge soaking up every aspect of our environment. We absorb our parents' behaviours, teachers' influences, and every facet of our surroundings. If our parent's express anger over trivial matters, we will likely do the same. The energy and vibrations we experience as happy newborns may not be the same as what we encounter 15 to 20 years later. Suppose a prevalence of anger marks our upbringing. In that case, we're likely to carry that energy into adulthood, becoming individuals who react angrily even to minor issues, not even realizing to whom we are projecting our anger.

This pattern continues to shape not only our behaviours but also our self-identity. As we go through the different stages of life, we often become very connected to the outside world and disconnected from our inner being.

Our daily tasks, responsibilities, and the steady flow of news and events take up all of our time. This way, we slowly relinquish our freedom and become slaves to our senses. We get up daily to deal with the things that need our attention. When we get to work, advancing our careers and maintaining financial security take priority. The desire for material things and the comforts they provide also occupy our thoughts. The more we interact with the outside world, the less time we have for self-discovery and reflection. Even when we're not working, we can be looking for new things to do, whether it's through trips, new purchases, delicious food, or other sensory treats. While there is nothing wrong with it, we need to focus on one thing, which is our identity, the real us, which no label outside of us can define; only we have the power to feel and live it.

Now, the meaning of "I" fluctuates throughout our lives based on what we acquire and become. When a person becomes a wife or husband and then a mother or father, their behaviour and thinking will alter to match the energy of their identity, which was created through the possessions they acquired. This identity also gives us a great deal of conceit.

Say that we instinctively smile when we see a baby, and that smile is one of innocence and purity. Because this infant does not recognize others by occupation or name, he recognizes them as pure beings because he is in a state of pureness. Even though the infant has not yet acquired anything, we find them attractive and love them as much as possible. Why? We see them as divinely perfect beings, and they see us in the same light. They will maintain the same manner of being regardless of who they interact with, the colour of their skin, or the type of clothing they wear. The opposite of how we interact with people as adults. As he grows older, he is also acquiring many things and is being taught not to give love as much as he did when he was young but rather to take from people, which is respect, love, and acceptance for what he has acquired in his life. This infant is no longer appealing because his innocence has diminished, and his ego has grown.

Even in all the stages of life, the child's body has gone through many stages. Many new labels have been put on him, but there was something in him that never changed and remained stable throughout his life. What is that thing? It is that immovable, unshakable, everlasting, ageless being that is powerful beyond measure.

But for us to understand it, we first need to be free from all the labels that we have allowed to define us. It is not easy to break free from the habits formed in us over billions of lives in which we only thought of ourselves as bodies. If we've grown to the point where we associate more with our minds and spirits, the body will still need most of our attention, energy, and a strong emotional bond. We do it without thinking about it, and it takes precedence over any feelings or thoughts that tell us to do something different.

Consequently, we must always say, think, and act in line with the phrase, "Ashes are the end of my body." This will sound upsetting or sad if we keep looking at our bodies as our identities. We are in a self-hypnotic state; what you and I see is different; this is just one reality. In another one, in that situation, it resembles an infinite, all-encompassing universe that has no limits. This reality consists of both things we understand and those unknown to us. In that instant, it is the only actual universe.

The existence of this soul, or Self, permeates all things and people. The name, shape, physique, and gender are all outside. But if we look past these distinctions, such as names and physical appearances, we find that there is only one thing in the world, which is energy. We, as souls, are also made of energy. You and I are one. The natural world and the universe do not exist; there is only one endless existence.

How can you tell who the knower is? It cannot be known. What do you think of yourself? The only one is the soul, an incomparably strong energy entity that cannot be destroyed or broken. Everybody and everything is part of it. It is not constrained by time or location.

It resides in our third eye, between our brows. It started there and controlled the entire body and psyche. When the soul enters the body, it reflects the personality traits accumulated from previous lifetimes in other souls. Who can reflect? You.

This entire cosmos is a reflection of the soul, an eternal being. As the reflection strikes either excellent or evil reflectors, it produces images of both the wonderful and the horrible. Therefore, a thief's reflector is built of negative energy, whereas a saint's reflector is formed of pure energy. By definition, the soul is pure. It is what gives life to a person; it fills his whole body, including his breath and prana, and it goes beyond his mind. The soul is left over when everything that isn't the Self is taken away.

Remember that the body, life, feelings, thoughts, mind, and intellect are not the same thing as the part of a person that was not born and will live forever.

To be clear, these are not the Self; they are just how it looks to other people. Our true selves are nothing but pure existence, knowing ourselves and not having any mental or intellectual structures that hold us back. When we take our minds off of everything going on in the outside world, we have an experience that is strange, amazing, and deep.

Being self-aware is a fantastic thing in and of itself; the soul is, by definition, pure. For us to understand it, it takes some time due to our conditioning of being body-conscious since we were born. The mind cannot shine a light on the Self because it is naturally divided into subject and object.

People who can see themselves in others and others in themselves can help others see who they are. Those who are wise have become aware of it through meditation. The everlasting Self, beyond all knowledge, is hidden in the heart cave. To find it, you have to give up both pain and pleasure— people who are aware that they are not their thoughts or bodies. The eternal Self, on the other hand, is the divine principle of being. Its roots may lie in its source, filled with joy and happiness. The Self that knows everything was never born and will never die. This Self does not change and will never change. It is not affected by causes and effects. The Self comes back to life even after the body dies. The Self is at the heart of all living things. It is more potent than the most powerful and more complex to see than the easiest to see. The soul is something we should get to know and appreciate. It's like our true selves. But just getting to know ourselves isn't the final step. We should also aim to experience the "Paramatman," which is like the Self of our inner Self. This might sound like we're transcending ourselves, but really, it's about understanding that the highest Self and ourselves are the same.

Sometimes, people think that all they need to do is focus on themselves, and that's enough. They believe that getting in touch with themselves is the ultimate goal. But this is a misleading idea. It's essential to remember that our personal growth goes beyond just understanding ourselves. Some people might even think that if they could erase their existence, they would reach a state of enlightenment, or perhaps they would realize that there is no image and no one to perceive it. But this belief is dangerous—a way of thinking that suggests no meaning or value in anything. It is a trap we should avoid. In essence, it's about understanding that our true selves and the highest selves are interconnected, and our personal development is a journey that goes beyond our existence.

For many, to hear of the Self is something they have yet to do.

By far, most people have never heard of the Self, and they never will in their entire lives. What kind of spirit it is as a part of the Supreme Being and, therefore, an essential part of it. Will makes reality and, consequently, supreme reality itself, which never ends, never dies, and can't be split up. They won't be told anything about it or even think of it themselves. Another thing is that the spirit won't even be able to approach them from inside or outside the group. Nature is nothing but the Self; it is the only true identity they will ever have. Being unchangeable means that this Self can't be changed by anything, not itself. God included. Both things cannot be changed; they are what they are.

Therefore, it is not only the activity that is best for us to do, even though it is the only one we can take part in some way. Everything else is made up of illusions.

"Creation is only the projection into form of that which already exists."

Shrimad Bhagavatam (9th Century)

Ancient Hindu Text

This beautiful understanding of the Self must be the only window we use to look at what is happening in the world now. Many souls are going through the development process at the same time. Being able to have an experience of oneself in one's own right: When a person breathes, they are conscious of him as the breath; when they speak, they are mindful of him as their voice; when they see, they are conscious of him as their eye; and when they hear, they are aware of him as their ear; and when a person thinks, they can recognize him as the mind.

Even though there is a dizzying array of names and shapes all around us, we must never forget that they are ultimately nothing more than the One, the Self, that we are all a part of by internally going over our thoughts and going over them repeatedly. We will be able to transcend both name and form by cultivating the practice of meditation to become aware of the One.

This will allow us to become anchored in consciousness and firmly established there. If someone who holds the Self in high regard says to someone with something else in higher regard than the Self, "(what you hold) dear will perish," that person is undoubtedly capable of making such a statement, and it will indeed come to pass. Meditation should only ever be done on oneself, realizing that we are one with the universal consciousness, as this is the most important thing. Those who dwell on themselves alone find that they are not subject to death. The Self is always closer to us than anything else could be.

Therefore, rather than looking for it by looking outward, we should look inward to find or perceive it. It is the thing we hold dearest because it is ourselves and the only thing we can ever have; everything else in the world is an illusion that will eventually fade.

Those who focus their attention away from themselves and onto objects in the external world will, as a result, discover that everything they care about eventually passes out and is no longer accessible to them. Because of this, valuing oneself above all else is not only a sign of high moral character; it is also sound advice. Adopting any other perspective is a symptom of being body-conscious. Other symptoms include attaching our identity to our body, achievements, etc. We can conquer death if we base our lives on the idea that we are immortal and work toward that goal.

Everything else in the universe is considered unreal, having been manifested and manufactured by the force of illusion or ignorance, asserting that there is only one thing tangible in the universe, which it calls the soul. If we can overcome this ignorance, then we will finally be able to see ourselves as we indeed are. The body is the exterior covering, and the mind is the inside coating of the soul. The soul is the true perceiver, the true enjoyer, and the entity that resides in the body and controls it through the use of the mind or an internal organ. Because it is immaterial, the soul cannot be limited; because it is not limited, it does not obey the rule of cause and effect; therefore, it is immortal. It is the only entity in the human body that is immaterial.

Because everything that has a start also must have an end, that which is immortal must have always existed without a beginning. There cannot be any shape without matter; the logical conclusion is that it must be formless. Everything that can be described as having shape must have a starting point and a conclusion. No one among us has ever witnessed a structure that was without a beginning and will never be without an end—the interaction of force and material results in the formation of a form.

Let's take the example of a chair as an illustration. We can see that chairs have a distinct form because a certain amount of matter is subjected to a specific amount of force, which causes the matter to assume a particular shape due to the interaction between the two.

Anything that occupies space that our senses can perceive is matter, and it takes force for matter to occupy space. And behind every existence, the same force is required: energy.

The form is the result of the interaction between matter and force. The combination cannot last forever; eventually, as is the case with all combinations, it will fall apart. This is an impossibility. Therefore, there is a start and a finish to all forms.

We know that our physical form will eventually pass away because everything has a beginning and an end. It has been around for an unlimited amount of time, and, in the same way that time itself is eternal, so too is the Self of a person.

Second, it must be all-encompassing and all-pervasive. Form is the only thing that can be constrained and conditioned by space; formlessness, on the other hand, cannot be contained. Therefore, the Self, also known as the soul, is present in everyone. This includes both you and me. You are currently in the sun just as much as you are on this earth, and you are in England just as much as you are in the United States.

However, the Self exerts its influence through the intellect and the body, and wherever these two components are, the Self's activity may be observed. Every action we take and every idea that goes through our heads leaves an imprint, referred to as a samskara in Sanskrit. The accumulation of all of these samskaras culminates in the powerful force that is our character. A man's character is composed of qualities that he has developed both in this life and in previous incarnations. It is the consequence of the mental and physical activities he has engaged in throughout his life. The sum of an individual's samskaras is the driving force that determines the path an individual takes after death.

When a person passes away, their body disintegrates and returns to its origin, but their samskaras continue to exist and are attached to their mind. Because the mind is composed of such fine material, it does not disintegrate, as the finer the material, the more tenacious it is.

The soul is the master of the senses.

The Self does not move, but because it is constantly out of the reach of the searching senses, it is always in front of them. Referring to "not subjective experience, nor objective experience, nor experience midway between these two, nor is it a negative situation that is neither consciousness nor unconsciousness," according to the consciousness of the Self, It is not sensory knowledge, relative knowledge, or inferential information at this time. Beyond the senses, beyond comprehension, and beyond all means of expression, it is pure unified consciousness in which all awareness of the outside world and plurality is utterly eradicated. It is an unfathomable tranquillity. The highest good is it. Without a second, it is one. The Self is it. Only you know it!

There is the Self everywhere.

The Self is everywhere and nowhere simultaneously because it exists outside of time and space, depending on your perspective.

There is just one sure thing: the Self is never, to any extent, removed from and is always fully present. Given that, we need to become aware of the Self, not seek it. We constantly experience sight and touch, and although they exist within the Self, we are unaware of them, just as fish cannot perceive water due to its close and essential link to them.

The Self is more advanced for us than water is for fish. The easiest way to put this concept into practice is to be constantly aware of the Self and grounded, which can be accomplished through regular meditation. Being outside of the illusions of time and space.

The Self appears to move, yet it does not move.

Because the Self exists outside the illusions of time and space, it neither moves nor undergoes any change. The immobile witness momentarily experiences a plethora of externalities caught up in the film and, believing they are inside it, undergoes the change scenario.

Similarly, visualizing, seeing, or doing something differs from seeing or doing it. Doing it, and therefore witnessing the motion picture of many lives and their attendant joys and sufferings, is not the same as being born, lived, and died repeatedly.

It is within all, yet it is outside all simultaneously.

Nothing, not even an illusion, can exist independently of the Self. Even if it takes place entirely in the mind, a hallucination is nonetheless considered to be a "thing." The Self is the foundation that all else rests upon and exists inside. Everything endures, serving as a screen upon which the life-long play of light and shadow can be viewed.

It is, in and of itself, the foundation of all that can be viewed. From a certain point of view, it is possible to assert that everything contains a part of itself that is mindful of its existence. Given that they will never be connected, it is possible to speak of them as being outside of all things or as being foreign to all things. Whichever way you look at it, say it any way you like; the concept remains the same: the Self never interacts with any object.

Bodiless

It should come as no surprise that the Self is not composed of matter, but we need to understand that the 'Self' never interacts with materiality and that it does not possess a body in the traditional sense. A component that is incorporated into a body and either influences or is affected by it

engaged in a wide variety of activities, which, among other things, include intellectual study, and the only places where conceptualizations can take place are in the different bodies or koshas, and as a result, have nothing to do with the Self in any way, shape, or form and are therefore often irrelevant.

This is a fact. The bodies need to be cleansed and refined so that they no longer hide or obscure the Self, but we need to remember that the entire process occurs outside of the Self and never has any effect on the Self, not even slightly. It is also essential to understand that the Self is not actually "in" the body at any time. It cannot be encircled or confined by anything, including itself, due to the sheer nature of its existence. The human body The Bhagavad Gita quotes Krishna as saying,

"They are contained in me, yet I am not in them.
"Gita 7:12"

And this is also true for our very own selves. For us to become conscious of the Self, we need to withdraw our awareness from our bodies completely. Even though during meditation, we use our bodies as stepping stones to reach a higher state of consciousness, approach the Self, and ultimately overcome the body consciousness completely, a point will come where we can't reject it.

Pure

The Self is also called "pure" because nothing stands in the way of the Self's connection with anything else, including our connection to the divine. It is complete and lucid, devoid of any admixture.

The seer/observer

The Self is the unwitnessed witness. Since the senses, the mind, and the intellect are merely energy creations; there is no other witness at the individual level that lacks personal consciousness. The ear cannot hear what the sight cannot see. No longer do the intellect or brain. Instead, it is the spirit of consciousness. Witness their messages; therefore, the Upanishad seer said,

"The self is the ear of the messenger."

The ear, the thinking, and the speech It is also the eye of the eye and the breath of the breath. After letting go of the delusion that the Self is connected to the senses and the mind and realizing that their Self is the infinite, the knowledgeable, they become one with divine union when they leave this existence.

The end of ignorance

Matter is subject to decay. The Lord, also known as the one who rids the world of ignorance, is unending and immortal. It is the only universal awareness that resides in every one of us, and it reigns supreme over everything that has the potential to perish.

By way of meditation on that, by affiliating oneself with it, and by associating oneself with that, one stops being what one was. This vast cosmos is a wheel. On which all souls go through the cycle of birth, death, and rebirth. It continues to go in circles without ever coming to a stop. It is the axis upon which our soul is. It will continue to rotate as long as the individual Self believes it is distinct from the infinite source. Upon the wheel in subservience to the rules governing birth, death, and reincarnation. But, after all of that, through the favour of the source, it comes to understand that it is identical to it; it turns on the wheel without stopping longer. It attains the status of immortality". Time, space, law, chance, matter, primal energy, and intelligence—none of these, nor a combination of these, can be the final cause of the universe, for they are effects and exist to serve the soul. Nor can the individual Self be the cause, for being subject to the law of happiness and misery is not free. This Self, which is pure consciousness, is God and all gods.

It is also the five elements—earth, air, fire, water, and ether—as well as all beings, significant and tiny, born of eggs, born from the womb, born from heat, and from the soil. The reality that lies underneath all of these is soul energy, which is just consciousness in its purest form.

The Self is unknown; all three states of the soul—waking, dreaming, and dreamless sleep—are nothing more than dreaming. Each of these is a location where the Self can be found: while we are awake, the Self resides in the eye; when we are asleep, the Self lives in the mind; and when we are dreaming, the Self resides in the heart's lotus.

This is because we are ignorant. We also consider that they are the forces causing us to behave or think in the manner we do, as well as the effects they have on us.

Astral Body

When awake and conscious, the physical body, including the physical brain, dominates our awareness. However, when we are dreaming, it is the astral body that comes into function and takes the reins of our consciousness.

This astral body separates from the physical body upon death; therefore, it is commonly confused with the spirit self by many people who believe in life after death.

The ancient Rishis of India have a high degree of credibility. We need to take it one step further. There is also another facet to consider with this.

The astral body is where emotions and many other feelings are stored.

"'There are two states for a person: the state in this world and the state in the next; there is also a third state, the one intermediate between these two, which can be likened to dreaming."

When a person is in the intermediate states, they will experience all other states, both this world and the next. This will happen in the following way: after death, they continue to exist only in the subtle body, which bears the memories of their past lives. Past deeds and the pure light of the current moment light up these imprints, and he is conscious of them.

Once more, while he is in this transitional state, he can view both the misfortunes and the good fortune that will still come to him based on his decisions and choices. Behaviour, both positive and negative that people exhibit on the surface of the earth

We have bodies and are physically present, or we have no bodies and dwell in the astral plane. However, between these two states is the dream state, in which we experience both material and cosmic conditions simultaneously. For instance, we go over the edge of a cliff and feel falling in the same way that we would in the state of being awake. But even though we collide with the ground, none of us will perish, and it won't even hurt because it is the astral world and not the physical plane.

In the astral world, things work out just like that. This is why young children are so brave and unafraid, as most children would rush headfirst into a potentially dangerous scenario without hesitating.

The transcendent Self

In actuality, the Self, in its authentic form, is free from covetousness, evil, and fear. A person in union with the Self, which refers to our connection with our higher or divine Self, knows nothing that is without, nothing that is within, because, in that condition, all of one's wishes have been fulfilled. When we are connected to our higher Self, all of our desires and wishes get dissolved because the reason for which we were chasing them diminishes.

The only thing that interests us is himself; devoid of aversion and suffering, it transcends both. Then the mother is not a mother, and the father is not a father; worlds dissolve, gods disappear, and scriptures disappear; the thief and the murderer are no more; neither a monk nor a hermit exists any longer. When this happens, the presence of evil does not affect the Self, and the heart's anguish will turn into joy.

"He neither sees, nor smells, nor tastes, nor speaks, nor hears, nor thinks, nor touches, nor knows; for there is nothing distinct from him; there is no second, "says the Buddha.

However, he is still able to see because he and the observer are one; he is also able to smell because smelling and he is one; and taste and he is the same; still, he can speak, for speech and he is the same; yet he can hear, for taste and speech is the same. This happens when we realize that all are energy the same.

The Self is eternal because it is the light of consciousness and immortal. After all, it is the Self.

"'When there is another, then one sees another, smells another, tastes another, speaks to another, hears another, thinks of another, touches another, and knows another.'"

"'When there is another, then one sees another, smells another, and tastes another.'"

Simple as the crystalline water is the Self; it is the only seer, and there is only one of them, which is the person's highest purpose, utmost wealth, and greatest happiness. It is the absolute centre of all things. Ignorant people can only experience a limited part of their limitless essence.

MEDITATION

Getting Ready for Meditation: Find a peaceful, comfortable place before we start. Remain relaxed and either sit or lie down. Breathe deeply for a few moments, slowly inhaling through your nose and out through your mouth.

Permit yourself to release the tensions and anxieties of the day. Keep your breath in mind. Shut your eyes and concentrate on your breathing.

As you inhale, sense the cool air entering your nostrils; as you exhale, feel the warm air exiting your body. Let your breathing find its own organic, effortless rhythm. Watching Your Ideas: You might get ideas while you're still breathing. Be judgment-free and let them come and go.

See these ideas as fleeting clouds in the big sky of your awareness. Once you've acknowledged them, let them go.

Pulling Away from Your Body: Start examining your body now. Work your way up to the top of your head, starting from your toes.

Imagine that each body part is detached from the others. Imagine yourself seeing your body from a distance and experiencing a release of stress.

Abandoning Labels: Consider all the designations you have given to yourself, such as roles, accomplishments, and work titles. Imagine these labels as stickers on your body, then carefully peel them off one at a time. Feel lightness and freedom as you take off each label. Getting in Touch with Your Real Self Imagine now that an energetic ball of white light is growing between your eyebrows.

This is who you are at your core.

Please pay attention to this energy and the sense of alienation it evokes. Consider it to be the focal point of your awareness. Combining with All Energy:

Imagine a stream of all-encompassing energy emerging from the universe and passing through the crown chakra at the top of your head. This energy unites with your authentic Self, reinforcing your bond and reaffirming your sense of separation. Giving Up Attachments Imagine that the tags and attachments you've cut off from your body are vanishing into the universe. They no longer burden you; instead, they merge with your boundless energy. Experience the freedom that this release brings.

Revealing in Who You Are: Take time to be with yourself without labels or attachments. Feel the calm, clarity, and sincerity that accompany this epiphany.

An Appreciative Attitude: Remember to be grateful for your connection to your true Self and the assistance of the universal energy as we get to the end of this meditation.

After inhaling deeply, a couple more times, open your eyes slowly when ready.

Every time you practice this meditation, you'll feel progressively lighter, enabling you to live authentically and act according to your true nature. This will be highly advantageous for everyone you are connected to and for you, as we are all energetically connected to a higher dimension.

Aura

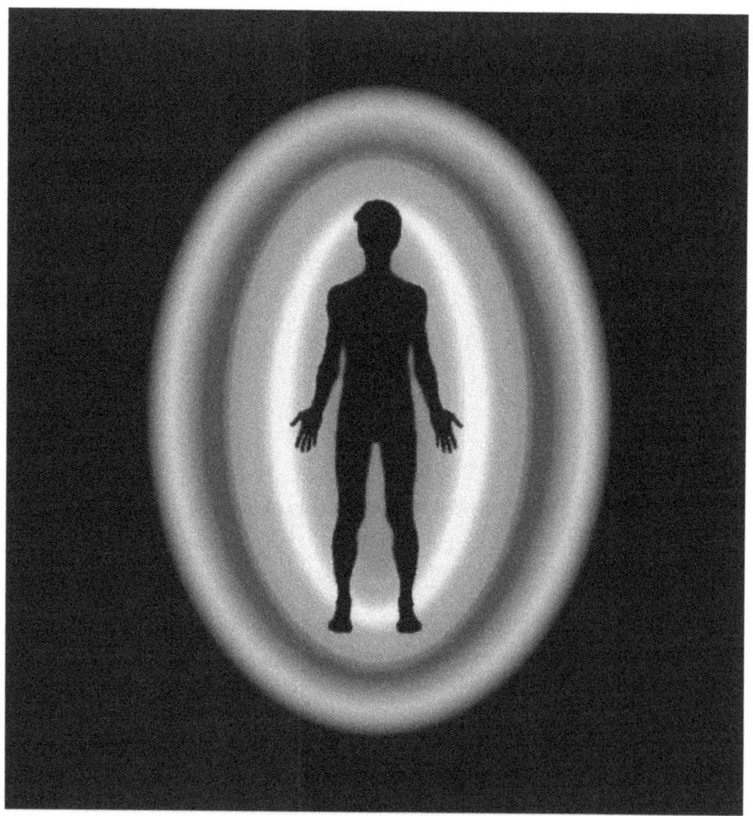

Aura of a Human Body

A soul can be described as having an aura, a brilliant and ethereal energy field that contains its essence. This ethereal sheath of light goes beyond the body to reveal the inner workings of a person's mind and heart. This ghostly cloak comprises a complex web of colours, patterns, and vibrations, all of which will be discussed in the upcoming chapter on auras.

A person's aura is like a kaleidoscope of the soul; it contains an immense amount of data about their personality, state of mind, and spiritual development. As we learn about auras, we'll discover their hidden meanings and significance, illuminating the relationship between our true selves and the multi-coloured cloaks we wear. This will allow us to appreciate the bond between the soul and its aura.

An aura, also known as an energy field or an unseen emanation, surrounds all living beings and can be thought of in either of these ways. Because some energy field encompasses everything, even inanimate objects like rocks or even tomatoes can have their unique auras. The aura, even though it encircles the totality of the body and reflects all the subtle life forces, is also contained within every cell of the body. This is the case even though the aura is said to be reflective of all the subtle life forces. As a result of this, it is possible to consider it to be nothing more than an extension of the body itself as opposed to anything that surrounds it. This is because it does not have a separate identity from the body.

The name aura may be traced back to the Greek word *avra*, which means "breeze."

This is also where the English word "aura" comes from. The energies circulating within our auras can convey information about our identities, how we live our lives, the thoughts, and sensations that we have, and so on.

A clear picture of our mental, physical, and spiritual well-being may often be gleaned from observing our academic fields. There are a significant number of people who believe that the aura is nothing more than an electromagnetic phenomenon and that it should be ignored because of this belief. The spark of life and our higher consciousness, which are supposed to supply us with the energies we need to exist and operate properly, are thought to be contained within it by some people who also believe that it houses our higher awareness. Still others maintain that the aura is nothing more than a mirror of the person and that, because of this, it includes a whole history of the person's past, present, and even future.

It is a combination of all of these different aspects working together. The vast majority of researchers working in this area think that every one of us possesses what is known as a physical aura. This is made up of the material that makes up the body in addition to the energy fields that are all around it. Temperature discrepancies can be observed between people and their settings because, on average, people have a higher core body temperature than their surroundings.

As a direct result of this, there will be air currents that are relatively close to our bodies. When at rest, our bodies give off a radiation known as infrared that can be detected from a distance. In addition to this, electrical ion fields and electrostatic fields are constantly present all around us. In addition, we also emit minute amounts of electromagnetic radiation in the form of radio waves and low-frequency radiation with a frequency of up to one hundred kilocycles. These waves and radiation have a frequency of up to one hundred thousand cycles per second.

Specific individuals could see auras at various points in history.

Nowadays, in recent years, aura photography has attracted a lot of interest. This technique – *Kirlian photography*, which includes capturing the electromagnetic energy fields that are thought to surround living things using specialized cameras that have sensors built into them. These energy fields, often known as auras, are supposed to reveal information about a person's mental, emotional, physical, and spiritual well-being. This energy is translated into visible colours by the aura camera, and each colour has a distinct meaning. A blue aura, on the other hand, might represent intuition and serenity, while a red aura might represent physical vitality. Practitioners or aura readers frequently interpret aura photos, giving advice and insights into a person's relationships and health, among other areas of their life. In the spiritual and New Age circles, aura photography has grown in popularity. It is frequently seen at events, metaphysical expos, and holistic treatment facilities. For people curious about the relationship between energy, emotions, and spirituality, aura photography remains a fascinating and captivating field.

However, it was not until recent times that scientists were able to confirm the presence of this invisible "surround" that psychics have always been able to see. This "surround" is said to encircle everything in the universe.

Many people can sense auras when they are young, but as they get older, they lose it. Auras can be perceived in several distinctively distinct ways. In most situations, they are considered energy fields that wrap the body, much like a giant egg might.

Most auras wrap around the body for a distance of several feet. It is commonly held that a person's aura will expand in proportion to the degree to which they have developed their spirituality. For instance, people believed the Buddha had an aura that extended for several miles in every direction. The individual's mental processes, sentiments, health, and potential are reflected within this big egg's lines of power and energy, which radiate out in all directions and may be seen from within the egg. The energy fields that make up an aura all flow in a direction that is perpendicular to one another.

The first one moves in a vertical direction from the head down to the feet of the body. Energy fields go around the body in a direction that is horizontal and in a path that is perpendicular to this path.

 Last, other energy waves leave the spinal column and travel toward the edge of the aura's sphere of influence. They all cross paths with one another and generate a magnetic energy web that is densely woven. Every colour conveys a message, and that message can be interpreted in a variety of ways. The order of the primary colours follows the order of the rainbow, and you will quickly realize that each of the rainbow colours can be found within each of our auras. The order of the primary colours follows the rainbow.

A person's aura, on the other hand, may contain colours that aren't present in the rainbow.

Red Potential as a Representation of Leadership: Having something in this colour gives you much power. It provides the individual with a robust ego as well as a desire. To accomplish goals and attain success. This colour is typically relatively muted when a person is a child, particularly if the individual is pressured to conform to the expectations of their family. As a direct consequence of this, the aura may, at times, appear flat and congested. The expansion of the person's aura, which occurs as they reach adulthood and can support themselves financially and emotionally, is a sign that they are now able to perform the responsibilities that are expected of them.

People with a red background typically succeed in positions of responsibility and leadership because they possess the drive, enthusiasm, and charm to motivate others to achieve their goals. In addition to that, they have a kind and loving nature. The colour is red can also signify bravery in terms of one's body. Both anxiousness and a focus on one's interests are characteristics that are associated with the colour red.

Orange Potential: Compatibility and Working Together. You'll notice that the base colour in this design is orange, which represents a kind and compassionate hue. Individuals with an innate capacity for intuition, tact, and ease of social interaction. They can put others at rest and thus find themselves in situations where they need to "calm the storm." They are the kind of people who put a lot of thought into their actions, are grounded in reality, are capable, and always keep their eyes on the prize. Laziness and a "couldn't care less" attitude are the negative characteristics associated with the colour orange.

Yellow Potential: Capacity for original thought and intellectual understanding. Yellow is a passionate, exuberant, and variable base colour; thus, people with this colour tend to be quite outgoing. They have a sharp mind and enjoy entertaining others and delighting themselves. They are outgoing and social and delight in engaging in extended discussions on various subjects. They are eager to learn, but they tend to dabble in a wide variety of topics and only scratch the surface of each one rather than focusing on mastering one field to the fullest extent possible. Yellow's bad characteristics include an inclination to lie and a tendency toward cowardice.

Green Potential: Healing People who have green as their base colour are typically lovers of peace and make excellent natural healers because of this. Green is a tranquil hue. They are trustworthy, they cooperate, and they give generously. They may give off the impression of being calm and easy-going, yet when they believe it is necessary, they can become quite obstinate and unyielding. The only way to convince someone with a green background to modify their opinion is to convince them that the concept is theirs. Green's negative characteristics include being rigid and having a fixed point of view.

Blue Potential: Because of the generally upbeat and cheerful nature of this individual. The auras are typically very huge and vivid. They experience the same number of peaks and valleys as everyone else, yet they always seem to emerge from the valleys with a surprising degree of ease. People with blue as their background colour will always have a childlike spirit. They are genuine and trustworthy, and they almost always say what is most directly on their minds.

One negative aspect of the colour blue is that it may make it more challenging to carry out various tasks. They are often better at beginning things, frequently with a great deal of excitement, than bringing them to a good completion by themselves or with the assistance of others.

Indigo Potential: Taking on the responsibilities of others. Because this colour can occasionally look almost purple, identifying it as the ground colour can be challenging. They are more likely to work in fields related to humanitarianism since yellow is a warm colour that promotes healing and nurturing. They take great pleasure in lending a hand to those in need and are happiest when surrounded by the individuals they care about the most.

Indigo's failing quality is unwilling to accept "no" as an answer. These are the kinds of people who make it very simple for others to take advantage of them.

Violet Potential: Spiritual and Intellectual Advancement. There is a reason why bishops wear purple robes; it is not an accident. People whose ground colour is violet continue to grow spiritually throughout their entire lives. The degree to which they have progressed up to this point can be estimated based on the intensity of this colour within their auras. Many individuals whose ground colour is violet try to conceal this aspect of their character. This will not make them happy, and they will be aware that they are not maximizing the potential of their lives in the way that they should. As soon as individuals begin to learn new things and advance in their knowledge and wisdom, their auras start to expand and become brighter as well.

Violet has a negative character trait known as an air of superiority, which can be off-putting to other people. Idealism carries a silver lining. It is not common to find silver as the ground colour, although it is regularly seen as an accent colour— the presence of one of the other hues in auras.

People whose ground colour is violet are full of brilliant ideas, but unfortunately, most are impracticable. People in this category frequently lack motivation, which leads to them being dreamers rather than doers. When people finally find something that motivates them and inspires them to take action, it can be a source of great pleasure to watch the progress that they make.

Gold Potential: Unlimited. When used as a ground colour, this shade is, by and large, the most effective of all the options. Individuals who possess it can handle large-scale initiatives and can do almost everything they set their minds to. People who create goals for themselves are personable, patient, and hard-working. Late in life is typically when people enjoy their most significant levels of achievement. It should not be surprising that paintings of halos around saints and other spiritual beings are commonly depicted as being made of gold, as this colour is meant to convey endless potential.

Pink Potential: Financial and material success. This colour, which has the appearance of being delicate, is frequently used as the base colour of determined, stubborn people. They have lofty ambitions for themselves, and they pursue those ambitions with unyielding willpower. It is hardly surprising that they are often found in positions of power and responsibility. On the other hand, they are humble and unpretentious individuals who enjoy leading a quiet existence. They are also kind and loving, and they experience the most happiness when they are with those, they love the most.

Bronze Potential: Humanitarianism. This colour is typically associated with the fall season, and it has an almost rusty aspect. It can possess a startlingly alluring appeal. People whose base colour is bronze are kind, sympathetic, and charitable humanitarians. They have a kind disposition and are generous. As a consequence of this, individuals frequently have to learn how to say "no" since other people place unreasonable demands on them.

White potential: The ability to shed light and provide motivation. White is the most associated with cleanliness; however, it is rarely used as the base colour. Given that every single white is the starting point for colour, and white is essentially just another word for light, people who have this trait are humble, selfless, and self-effacing humanitarians. They frequently give off the impression of being completely devoid of ego and seem far more concerned with the well-being of other people than they are with their own. These individuals typically have a high level of intuition and are wise beyond their years.

One technique people occasionally use to try to evaluate their aura is called the "pendulum method." A pendulum, a weighted device suspended on a thread or chain, can get insight into a person's aura's hue or health.

If you wish to explore this technique, here's a general guide on using a pendulum for aura assessment.

Pendulum Method

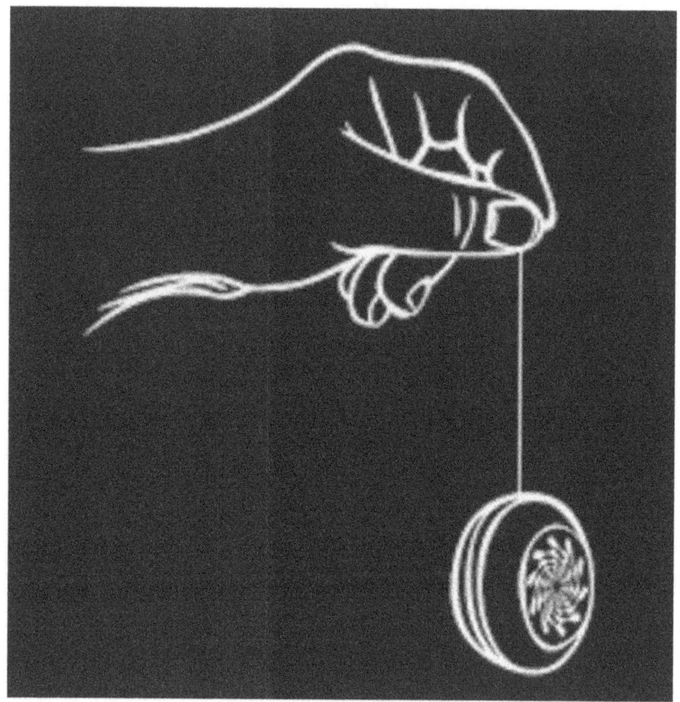

Pendulum

Method of Pendulum in Mediation: If you wish to use the pendulum method, locate a private area, sit silently, and speak to the pendulum about each chakra.

Beginning with the root chakra, ascend until you reach the summit chakra.

The first question you should ask using a pendulum is,

"Is my root chakra healthy? "

If the answer to this question is "yes," you may proceed to ask questions that pertain to your personal development.

You have the option of asking inquiries about restoration if the answer is no. This chakra is necessary for a healthy lifestyle. Let's assume the pendulum's response to the initial query was negative.

Then you query,

"Has my root chakra been activated too much?"

If the answer is yes, some measures can be taken to limit the excessive activity. If you receive a negative response to this inquiry, consider whether the chakra receives sufficient stimulation.

Again, if the answer to this query is "yes," then there is something that can be done to restore balance. It is widely held that the seven main chakras can be brought into harmony and balance by reciting specific mantras that match them. The seven chakras are central to many yogic and spiritual practices, and it is believed that reciting the mantras linked to each chakra will improve one's health on all levels. Listed below are the seven chakras and the mantras that correspond with them: "Lam" (or "Lahm" if you like) is a mantra for the first chakra, the root (Muladhara). It is thought that reciting the "Lam" mantra will make you feel more secure and stable. Mantra: "Vam" (pronounced as "vahm"). Sacral Chakra (Svadhisthana). The "Vam" mantra is said to bring about more fabulous inspiration, enthusiasm, and mental stability in its listeners. Third Chakra (Solar Plexus, or Manipura) Mantra: "Ram" (or "Rahm"). The "Ram" mantra increases one's sense of personal strength, power, and confidence—mantra for the Fourth Chakra (Anahata): "Yam" (pronounced "yam"). Love, compassion, and the healing of emotional wounds are claimed to result from chanting the "Yam" mantra. Mantra: "Ham" (pronounced as "hahm"). Throat Chakra (Vishuddha): Some people believe that repeating the mantra "Ham" will help them speak more clearly and honestly. Mantra for the Third Eye (Ajna) Chakra: "Om" (pronounced "ohm") or "Aum" (pronounced "a-uh-m"). By stimulating the third eye, chanting "Om" or "Aum" is thought to improve one's ability to tap into one's own innate wisdom and insight. Mantra: "Om" (pronounced "ohm") or "Aum" (pronounced "a-uh-m") for the seventh chakra, the crown (Sahasrara). Spiritual awakening and a connection to the universe are said to be facilitated by chanting "Om" or "Aum" at the head chakra. When reciting these mantras, it is crucial to concentrate on the corresponding chakra colour and see energy flowing freely clockwise within it. These mantras can be said during yoga or meditation sessions to improve one's health and happiness. Each chakra should be interrogated with the same set of inquiries. After completing everything, you can take whatever steps are necessary to restore the harmony of your chakras to see auras.

Aura Cleanse: Cleansing our physical body is important, as is cleansing our auric body. Our aura becomes tainted by external factors, just as our physical body does. Any physical illness affects our aura before it affects our physical body. If we cleanse our aura every day for fifteen minutes, we can be free of many diseases. Even if a disease has already entered our bodies, our negative thoughts, which weaken our aura, first affect it. This vulnerability then makes it possible for our aura to absorb the negative energy of other people. The first stage in clearing our aura is visualizing our hands as cleaners. Then, move them in all four directions from up to down while visualizing negative energy, such as rage, envy, greed, lust, etc., clearing our aura. It creates a pure aura and becoming pure through universal energy. Cleaning our aura can also be achieved by bathing in salt water.

Aura Lock: Negative energy is drawn to us while we are vibrating at a higher frequency, which eventually drains our energy. So that we can safeguard our energy there are methods that we can use to safeguard our energy.

First, before you leave the House, tell yourself aloud or in your head that your aura is locked, that no outside energy can enter it, and that my energy cannot leave it. It works by sealing your aura and shielding you from anyone who would wish you harm or from even a tiny amount of negative energy entering your aura.

The second technique is to visualize a line that runs from your root chakra to your crown chakra, then from left to right. You have now secured your aura, making it impossible for anyone to have a negative or positive influence on your frequency. Once we leave for work, we can utilize any of these techniques to help protect ourselves against both physical and emotional infections from other people.

CHAPTER 2

KARMA

What exactly is karma?

Karma is the principle that governs this universe of becoming. Karma and fate are closely related. Karma is the energy we send into the world, while destiny is the energy that comes to me from the outside. If we have a thought for another person, it will create our karma, which will be our fate. It is similar to firing an arrow that returns to us. When we fired that arrow, it was our karma, and when it returned, it was our fate.

Throughout our day, we fire an arrow that returns to us, creating and living our destiny. The equation is functioning throughout the day. In addition to physical regulations, there are also moral and spiritual laws. If we disobey the laws of health, it will negatively affect our health; if we violate the laws of mortality, it will negatively affect our higher existence.

Any reasonable conception of the universe, as well as any spiritual conception of deity, requires us to recognize the absolute and unquestionable pre-eminence of law in determining our actions and who we are as individuals. The principle of karma does not operate independently of individuals. The adjudicator resides not outside of us but within us. The law that governs how virtue and good deeds are rewarded is not triumph, and the law that regulates how evil deeds are punished is our own being's law.

The divine intelligence is reflected in the order of the universe. The mechanism by which karma operates is entirely emotionless, impartial, and neither cruel nor merciful. Even though we cannot avoid the consequences of applying this principle, there is still cause for optimism: if man is what he has made of himself, then he can make of himself whatever he desires. Even when the spirit is at its most hopeless, it is unnecessary to abandon your faith completely.

Even if we travel in the incorrect direction, we are not doomed to an eternity of suffering. There are other states of existence through which we can advance our comprehension of the inexhaustible spirit with the unshakeable conviction that we will ultimately reach this destination. The only thing that occurs when one existence gives way to the next is a change in dreams.

The physical body and the grosser pranic bodies perish when the stored life force (a type of karma) for life is depleted; this is analogous to how a battery's charge is. From the tree, the subtle body also separates from the physical body and begins its voyage away from it—a procedure that results in a second birth on Earth, this time with a new body. During the period between births, the individual spends time in the astral realms, where the soul frequently does nothing but aimlessly wander and squander time. Sometimes, it is learning and growing so that its next existence will be significantly more successful and experienced than the previous one.

The time spent in this transitional state could range from a few hours to decades or even millions of years.

This is the exact karma responsible for everything. It's depleted and eventually fails. And just as the fruit is plummeting to the ground, it is ripe. It is described as what we do returning to us. It doesn't matter if it is pleasant or negative; it will return to us similarly.

 For example, let's take someone's money in a previous life and be unable to return it. A circumstance may arise in this incarnation in which someone may ask for money, or a criminal may violently take our money, or we were supposed to give someone 1 dollar instead of 100 dollars. It was the same money that we still need to return.

This is only one example. Imagine our entire life unfolding this way, with every person we meet and every event influencing our future fate.

Even astrological charts are subject to the effects of our previous karmic actions. Karma manifests itself not only in actions but also in thinking. Say you are furious at someone and want to do something to make them see their error but cannot. But if you have negative thoughts about them that are detrimental, you are building a karmic record.

Now, until we see them again in this or the next life, our opinions about each other will be based on the thoughts we sent them the last time. If we had sent them negative thoughts, they would not like us for no reason when we met, and vice versa. This happens when we meet someone, and we don't want them for no reason, and we may not even know why, and we say to ourselves,

"I don't know why; I just don't like them."

It can also happen in the reverse direction; we may meet someone and think,

"We just match each other's vibe so easily! "

Everything is dependent on our connection with them in previous lifetimes. Every idea influences our future fate. For to, we may occasionally ask ourselves,

"Why did this happen to me?"

Why would someone I had so much faith in betraying me in such a way? Sometimes, we do a lot of work and put in a lot of effort for something, but we need to be recognized for it, or worse, someone else gets all of the credit. These are only a few simple instances. It goes far deeper than that.

To comprehend it, we must first recognize that we are responsible souls. Our karmas affect not only us but the entire globe. It is one of the most important duties we have as the supreme soul. If we do not have a peaceful family, a quiet life, or profound inner peace, we may be sure that our karmas are insufficient to allow us to live a peaceful life.

First, we must distinguish between excellent and low-quality karma. Many people believe that karma is either good or harmful and that it prevents us from being free. Some believe it is also an old, archaic way and some form of demonic activity. When in reality, it has nothing to do with this assumption and goes much beyond it. This notion prevents individuals from creating high-quality karmas and keeps them trapped in this three-dimensional realm.

It is causing them to reincarnate and be involved in unending issues repeatedly. They are then unable to locate a way out. Our liberation begins with realizing the truth, and if that is difficult to accept, then try it for yourself.

As you read and comprehend, begin implementing it in your life right away. It all comes back to us in the way we think about others. In general, we are always focused on others and how they act and think about us. Our happiness should never be dependent on the actions of others. High-quality karmas consistently outperform low-quality karmas.

We were aware of our genuine nature in ancient times, nearly thousands of years ago. We were mindful of our true nature and strength. We were both the creators and the destroyers. All of our psychic senses were heightened. All of the powers that seem unbelievable now, like teleportation and telepathy, were once commonplace in our daily lives. Our nature was pure, and we never relied on others for happiness and peace. There was no real distinction between God and us. Everything was in balance; nature was in harmony. We never created technology because we did not need it. No one needed the feeling of robbing or harming anyone in our civilization since we were conscious of our genuine nature of peace, purity, and contentment. Earth was a paradise. It would help if you now had a better understanding of our true nature and strength. We were the gods and goddesses to whom we prayed, but our heavy baggage of karmas and thoughts bound us to lower energies and kept us behind an illusionary wall.

"Karma" is derived from the Sanskrit word "*kri*," which means "to do." Every action is regarded as karma. This term can also refer to the outcomes of actions.

Sometimes, in metaphysics, the term refers to the effects. They were the consequences of our previous actions. In Karma-Yoga, however, we are only concerned with the notion that karma can also mean labour. The pursuit of knowledge should be the goal of humanity. This is the ideal the Eastern philosophical tradition has presented to us.

Man's purpose is not to pursue pleasure, but it is erroneous to believe that attaining enlightenment is the primary objective. The source of every ailment that befalls us is greed. The problem in this world is that, for whatever reason, people regard pleasure as the ultimate aim of their efforts. After some time, they realize that happiness is not what they believed it to be. But knowledge, for which he strives, and the realization that both pleasure and suffering are excellent teachers and that they have as much to gain from bad as they do from good as a consequence of sound—as happiness and suffering approach his consciousness, they bring with them a variety of images, the final product being a combination of these. rather knowledge.

Eventually, the enjoyment and contentment will cease. It is a dreadful situation.

Leaving the body (death):

"'When his body weakens and he appears to sleep, the dying man gathers his senses around him and, completely withdrawing their abilities, falls," according to the book "When a Man Dies." He no longer recognizes any shape or colour outside of himself.

He has no sight, no smell, and no taste. He doesn't speak, and he doesn't hear. He does not think, so he is unaware. Because his organs have disengaged from his body, you can unite your physical body with his subtle body.

Then, at the location of the nerves in his chest, he joins and receives the light of the self, and using that light, he either leaves through the joint or the light of the self. When he dies in this style, life ceases to exist, and when life ceases to exist, all vital system operations cease to exist as well. The principal has departed. The self remains conscious, and the dying man remains aware as he walks through his dwelling.

The actions we take in this life, as well as the impressions we leave behind, follow us into the next. When we engage with the material world, our thoughts and bodies serve as masks for our true selves, our souls. When we die, we shed our masks and our bodies and return to our original condition of consciousness. There is no such thing as disappearing or being forgotten.

Simply put, we shed our masks and facades. We shed our skin, hair, identity gained throughout our lives, and other exterior coverings and return to the spiritual world. Here, we can regain our strength and Vigor. We consider the life experiences that have moulded us in this section. We just got out. We are brought back together with the folks with whom we have shared our centuries in this place.

We plan our next existence on Earth from this vantage point.

When the timing is right, and we have put on our new masks—a baby's body and brain—we can return to the physiological state you were in. We are moving forward with newfound enthusiasm and optimism and improving our spiritual development to the point where reincarnation is no longer required to achieve our aims.

We will then be able to continue supporting people on the other side. It is critical to remember that the masks we wear do not represent who we indeed are; we are souls. We are moving forward with renewed zeal and excitement.

Improving our spiritual development to the point where reincarnation is no longer necessary to fulfill our goals will allow us to continue assisting those on the other side. It is vital to remember that the masks we wear do not represent who we are; we are souls.

Understanding can be sudden—a distinct and intuitive knowledge of the significance and meaning of these ideas. Understanding can also be gradual and deliberate, similar to a percolating consciousness as the veil of ignorance is gradually lifted. The results are the same whether you approach it with Zen-like immediacy or with the gradual rise of the light on a hazy day. Many obstacles stand in the way of our clear understanding.

When we are too young to comprehend, reason, or make decisions for ourselves, we are frequently force-fed specific cultural and religious belief systems. We may become disdainful of other viewpoints and systems. A closed mind is incapable of receiving information. There is nothing new that can be discovered. The act of giving birth in the astral world is deliberate.

We have the mistaken belief that we are weak and have no influence until we are incarnated on Earth or in the dark astral worlds. That explains why the leech analogy is used, as well as why the original Sanskrit language implies that humans are similar to leeches. Could you make a new form for ourselves? This also happens during a person's rebirth on Earth.

We choose where and to whom we will be born, and then we enter the womb of our determined mother and create our next physical home using the materials that both of our parents have provided. Our karma and samskara (nature) reveal the extent to which we are all powerful and intelligent. Are.

In the higher realms, the individual creates a body that is appropriate for the planet on which he will reside until the time comes when he wilfully undergoes rebirth. This is done to prepare for the hereafter. This experience will prepare him to create his body on Earth even faster and more effectively than before when he returns.

How can we heal our karmic patterns? Our lifetimes of karmic relationships are still with us, like baggage on our heads, slowly dissolving each day and making us feel good and bad at times.

Our happiness and sadness are all determined by what occurs to us, and what happens is our fate, which is determined by karma. Someone unaware of their true selves and the importance of their thoughts, words, and deeds is living this detailed life. It gets increasingly difficult for them to escape this dumb trap.

It becomes difficult for them, even though the truth is the opposite. Realization is the first step towards healing. The realization of ourselves—every speck of ourselves, every component of ourselves—has been suppressed for countless lives. For novices, it is not feasible to realize everything at once; the best approach to begin is to become aware of the feelings that are currently being felt. The thoughts in your mind, and if you want to delve further, write about the current events in your life. Our task now is to dismantle and resolve the karmic links.

Doctors all over the world are reporting an increase in medical situations, with some even claiming that the cure is often beyond their control. These high-rise situations are the result of our karma. Some people pass a competitive test on their first attempt, while others fail on their third. All of this results from our karmas manifesting themselves in our daily lives. Low-quality karmas are those that deplete our strength or energy. Those karmas that destroy our enjoyment, those karmas that drive us to be angry—that is why, to be free, meditation and forgiveness are required.

Some believe that karmas cannot be modified and that we must bear their consequences; while true, we can reduce their intensity to some extent. That is why we practice so many meditations.

High-quality karmas include blessing, loving, and respecting others and oneself. That is why, in any religious or spiritual teaching, one of the fundamental principles is to love and not hate anyone constantly. They always taught us to cultivate positive relationships with others and ourselves because anyone who causes us pain sends us negative energy that follows us into the next incarnation.

And, as a result of the karmic bond, it gives us difficulties at work or in relationships. Patients who had no prospect of survival began the forgiveness meditation after learning about karmic ties and realizing their condition was the outcome of their earlier karmas.

What is a karmic wound?

The great majority of people have a traumatic childhood as a result of experiencing at least one sort of emotional suffering during their childhood. It can sometimes get so bad that it manifests as a physical condition.

Some people may have a shallow level of trauma intensity, while others may have a very high level of trauma intensity. We are subject to a range of hazards when we are young, some of which may result in traumatic events. Someone will probably mistreat us. It is feasible that we will run out of resources to live—a lack of food supply due to economic hardship. Having no friends and spending time alone makes us the grown-ups we become.

Our childhood experiences and the ideas we developed as a result of how we perceived those events influence everything we do, from how we think to how we walk to how we work. Now the question is, why do we exactly experience those things while some people do not? Even when born as twins, many times only one twin experience certain feeling while the other does not feel anything traumatic at all in comparison to their brother or sister. This occurs as a result of our karmic relationships and baggage.

Which of the heaviest ones we were dealing with at the time manifested themselves in our youth, primarily between the ages of 4 and 7? At this age, our brain shifts into a different condition as karmic baggage manifests when we vibrate with the frequency of material vibration.

Except in rare cases where the karmic load is so powerful that it overwhelms the field and the infant in their pure state. All of our childhood experiences, particularly those that had the most significant impact on us, are the product of how we felt at the time of our previous life's demise.

For example, a child may feel very alone even though he has been included in events, has friends, and has excellent parents, but that youngster still feels alienated and unloved. This is likely because that is how the soul felt in its most recent costumes at the time of death. If we look at it practically, this is a relatively simple notion to grasp.

A former life regression can help you understand this better. It just takes a lot of concentration, and anyone can do it. If you cannot do so, you can seek healers and practitioners to assist you. But here, we just need to accept this and stop blaming our parents, our environment, our friends, and our teachers for the trauma we experienced as children.

Many people are unable to let go of prior painful experiences because they are unable to forgive. The main concerns that prevent them from recuperating are:

"Why me?"

"What did I do to deserve this? "

This "why me" question is so harmful that when we are unable to discover solutions to it, our subconscious minds create the explanation for us along the lines of

"I must be bad."

"That's why they treated me like that."

"There must be something wrong with me."

"I don't deserve love and appreciation,"

"I don't deserve to be great or happy,"

"I am a bad person and don't deserve anything good."

Our subconscious mind accepts all these explanations, and we live our lives accordingly, wondering why we are unhappy. All our difficulties and ideas that prevent us from being fulfilled and happy begin in infancy. This is how everything is intricately linked.

How our former life influences our childhood and subsequently our life, and how it affects our next life if we are not cured. It's a never-ending cycle of suffering that only degrades. Now, for us to be healed, we must first realize this without judgment.

We often criticize ourselves for doing something awful to someone, which then comes back to haunt us, making us a nasty person. When, in fact, it is quite the opposite.

Observing the present moment and observing what is happening is a pattern of thoughts, circumstances, beliefs, or other life events; it can also be a person who appears in your life repeatedly and whom you can remember. What it does is tell us about the feelings and thoughts associated with it that have yet to be healed.

Once you have identified these feelings, write them down or record them on your phone while saying them aloud. Whatever you want. However, stating your feelings out loud makes it much easier for them to realize.

If you feel unloved by your parents or instructors, you can state,

"I don't feel loved by my parents or teachers."

in the most genuine and specific way that you feel it. This will assist you in overcoming your feelings and putting them in a way that you can separate them and know what is causing you to feel this way, allowing the main feeling "stuck" to come to the surface and be healed.

 Allow the feelings to surface openly, even if they are frightening. Consider your brain to be a garbage can that is being emptied. All your profound wants, which you thought you could not live without, will go.

It will not cause any problems or give you the impression that you are missing out on something. We always see everything since our souls are already whole. It is our aspirations that keep us bound to the suffering plane. It doesn't mean you have to give up your desire to go to work tomorrow. Or, instead of shopping and traveling to new areas, change your mindset.

Be sure that all of the work that we require and the goals that we strive for are not motivated by a sense of "want" or "desire."

Even the law of attraction instructs us to "detach" from the emotion to obtain what we desire. The sensation behind our desires keeps us at a low frequency of want and pain.

Karma could reverse our roles.

Consider the possibility that you were once a thief who stole someone's money.

Now, in this life, you have acquired a lot of money through your hard work, but one day, by mistake, you give someone $100 instead of $10. You don't even realize it until you go home and realize what you've done, but now you're in a new city and have no idea where that spot is. You broke a karmic cycle.

This is known as reversing roles, with the person with whom we did it and then doing the same thing, though not in the same way, but with the same degree of feeling. It does not mean allowing crimes to occur and advocating for them, but it does mean not feeling like a victim when horrible things happen to us.

It is critical to understand and remember this because whenever something happens, we define ourselves as the victim, as we learned before. Many things have happened and will continue to happen to us that we believe are "unfair" yet are not. Nothing in this sophisticated creation is unjust.

We've all heard the expression, "Everything happens for a reason." It implies that what we did to them will be returned to us. If we steal anything from someone, our stuff will eventually be stolen. If we make fun of someone, they will ultimately make fun of us. These are only a few instances.

A lot of things happen that are difficult to accept and may leave you wondering,

"Did I even do that?"

Yes, you did.

The fact that things are occurring tonus indicates that we are in sync with that vibration, and we cannot be in tune with something we haven't felt or thought about. Even feelings and emotions are considered actions.

Because they, like action, contribute to the formation of our karmic relationship with someone. As energy can travel in all directions, the essential aspect to realize is that if someone does something to us that we believe is wrong, it is better to bless the one doing it. What it will do is that the energy we send them now will ultimately differ from what we sent them previously.

Science behind astrology

It reminds us that our actions have consequences, but it also specifies the time frame during which these consequences will manifest and the form they will take.

Let's imagine we read a prediction regarding the next day, and it says that we're likely to incur various losses today. If, after reading this, you agree with the author that losses are possible, then you are a walking, talking loss magnet. This will cause him financial harm in the long run.

Second, this foresight suggests we may have caused someone to feel as if they have "lost" something in the past by stealing it from them and that it is now returning to us. We have just scratched the surface here, but astrology can shed light on many life events, from relocation to a new nation to losing a loved one to our birth, which will make sense as we progress through this chapter.

The so-called growth of a soul that is given when used astrology becomes irrelevant when we realize that we, as a soul, have reached the pinnacle of our development and can go no further. We can learn about our karmic patterns from this, and if we cannot conduct past-life regression, astrology is a fantastic alternative for learning about our origins.

In this section, we shall discover the significance of each planet from our previous lives.

First, it's essential to realize that astrology isn't about personal development, as you've been told; instead, it subconsciously ties us down to destructive energetic patterns and karmic ties that might take a lot of time to overcome.

Consider another example: if an astrologer predicts that you will develop diabetes in six months, you have two options: you can either sit at home, or you can decide to adopt a healthier lifestyle and entirely alter your lifestyle. Now, after six months of a comprehensive dietary overhaul with no adverse effects, was this prediction accurate? Yes, but when I decided to alter my current behaviour, the future prediction changed.

Our current thoughts, words, and deeds have a significant impact on these astrological predictions, and we can completely alter them to the point where we no longer need to see or know about these things and can work in the manner we desire.

Here, however, we will delve deeper into these astrological planets to determine what they indeed signify and how they influence our karmic patterns so that we may heal completely.

The Planets: Each planet carries a karmic pattern to which we are connected.

SUN: Reveals the amount of vitality that the soul brings with it into this incarnation. Loss of a sense of self and devaluation of one's life are at the heart of karmic difficulties. It's possible that you're having trouble expressing yourself, and you may also feel an underlying yearning to reconnect with who or what our most fundamental source is.

MOON: carries a pattern of emotional behaviour that has been with them since childhood and is firmly imprinted. This sensitive planet reflects an individual's emotional blockages and their expectations of others through other individuals. There is a connection between the moon and the soul's picture of the mother and the feelings of maternal love carried from life to life.

MERCURY: It is a sign of karma associated with the mind, intelligence, thoughts, and logic. It explains how the soul communicates with other body parts and demonstrates how the mind was employed in the past. Additionally, it enlightens us regarding the karma that we share with our siblings and our relationships with them in our past lives.

VENUS: This connection is the medium via which it is communicated. It defines how a soul that has incarnated thinks about itself, including whether or not it believes it is deserving of love and what it holds most dear. It manifests itself in the form of karma through social contact. It also demonstrates how the eternal feminine has been expressed in various incarnations in the past.

JUPITER: This is the planet where everything is in excess. It demonstrates prior overindulgence in past lives and pinpoints the areas in which compensation needs to be provided. This planet has a connection to karma in both the secular and religious senses, as it is associated with travel and philosophy. If this planet's energy is blocked, the soul will no longer have the potential to create. Jupiter is linked to old cassettes from past incarnations, which must be reprogrammed to function correctly.

MARS: It demonstrates how assertive the spirit is in pursuing goals and aims. It describes experiences that people in the past have had with conflict and hostility. How much conflict and fury have impacted the person in the past, and how much they will continue to do so in the present.

NEPTUNE: It desires to be one with the divine once again. It embraces everything from the most significant stages of mystical and artistic consciousness to the realms of imagination and fantasy. It reveals karma connected to addictions and pain, as well as the places in the past when the soul attempted to avoid these things.

CHIRON: It reveals the area of the soul that is carrying a karmic wound, as well as the areas in which we have harmed ourselves, as well as the areas in which we have wounded others. This is the place where the soul needs to be healed, and it reveals the energies that need to be integrated. It shows the central scar left by previous lives.

Pluto has a connection with power and the entire cycle of birth, death, and rebirth. It is connected to all the soul has done to keep itself from seeing it. That needs to be eradicated, and it reveals where abuses and misuse of authority occurred. Additionally, it shows the necessity for soul empowerment.

Uranus: It feels the need to stand out from other things. The karmic awakener is the cycle of chaos and change that repeats itself. There is a connection between this karma and acts of disobedience and revolution. It is the place where the soul endeavours to introduce novel concepts and make use of an intuitive comprehension of the world. It is the planet of technology, and its presence might be interpreted as karma in this field. It can detect vibrations and bring them back into alignment to function correctly.

SATURN: To give our lives purpose and to provide them with some structure. Saturn prompts us to examine our commitment, sense of responsibility, and capacity for confinement by considering the limitations that matter and time impose on us. It details the debt responsibilities we had in our previous lives, both to ourselves and to other people. The burden that we were forced to bear for a tremendous number of lifetimes.

HOUSES: If a house does not appear to contain any planets, then it may appear to be empty. The position and aspects of the planet that dominate that House provide insight into its characteristics.

1st House: The first House reveals how the soul feels about entering embodiment and what it anticipates encountering on this journey through life. The sign on the ascendant illustrates how the soul travels out into the world to interact with it. For instance, a soul that Saturn rules enters this existence, anticipating that it will be challenging, especially during childhood. The job or obligation that is carried is the karmic weight that is taken. And if you're under the influence of Neptune, it can be challenging to see the soul that is incarnating. This soul must break through the delusions it has held onto from the past.

2nd House: This House manifests the karmic resources you brought back with you and the things you have developed in the years before moving in here. This House exemplifies the knowledge, abilities, and riches you have amassed throughout many lifetimes. They display their karmic resources by their inherent characteristics. For instance, if you have poverty consciousness and do not believe you deserve abundance, this could indicate that in a previous incarnation, you committed to live a life of poverty.

3rd House: If Saturn is in this House, it symbolizes a karmic restriction on communication, such as being deaf or having a throat chakra block. This House also represents the karma of siblings. The soul frequently experiences the experience of being exceedingly stupid, and as a result, it needs to reconnect with its natural intelligence one more time. If Pluto is there, it suggests a power struggle over what is and what has been, as well as conflicts among siblings. Neptune has difficulty feeling like it belongs on Earth or with its family, even if placed where it should be. This location exudes a sense of otherworldliness and estrangement from the rest of the world. Chiron almost always demonstrates that one of a sibling's wounds stems from their previous formal life.

The 4th and 10th Houses: This chart section contains the parental axes. It's a lesson in dealing with your parents' expectations and karma. Pluto is rife with political intrigue and power battles. Saturn is also heavy and may bring disappointment to the parent, or the parent may bring disappointment to Saturn. The soul does not expect to be recognized as an individual in its own right, nor is it appreciated as such. This soul educates itself to become its parent. Chiron may represent a parent who has been wounded or a home that has been damaged. The incarnated spirit anticipated having a difficult time as a parent.

5th House: The most crucial karmic placement in the fifth House which governs creativity. The presence of this planet suggests that there will be a delay or trouble in having a child or completing any other objectives. However, because the soul did not appreciate its creation in the past, it must now battle to come to terms with this.

6th House: The pursuit of happiness and maintaining a healthy lifestyle both lead one here. It does this in a very straightforward manner, bringing to light the karma of the body, which is the illness of the spirit. In addition, it indicates the continuation of a former profession in the direction of service or healthcare provision. Or a karmic obligation to rectify wrongdoing, such as performing some service.

7th House: This is the House of Relationships, and the karma involved was established in previous lifetimes and via those relationships.

8th House: The powerful karmic energy that radiates from this House makes it difficult to ascertain the significance of the information contained within it. Because it conceals its deepest, darkest secrets, in the context of this discussion, Saturn stands for the necessity of confronting one's fear of death. Pluto symbolizes an old conflict and the necessity to explore the cycle of life, death, and rebirth in various forms.

9th House: This is the House of Philosophy and Religion, and the karma linked with it can be dark and heavy, with a firm, immovable rigidity. This is the House that rules Capricorn. The karma came about because Uranus was trying to teach Neptune new ideas at a time when Neptune was developing a greater interest in spiritual matters. The soul has decided to atone for sins done in the past or to commit to a particular path of conduct to enhance its spiritual development. Both decisions might help the soul grow spiritually.

11th House: This House exemplifies the idea of karma as it relates to the functioning of groups and organizations. Since Uranus was brought to this location, the soul has worked toward establishing a revolution or a revolt. It has done what it can, through Saturn, to preserve its status in the community. Regarding Pluto, the disputes date back to antiquity and go on for a long time. Past illusions, delusions, and deceptions likely need to be atoned to go forward if Neptune is present. This is because Neptune symbolizes the unconscious mind.

12th House: When a soul is about to embark on the incarnation adventure, it stands on the ascendant and looks out around the circle of the chart. This is the most karmic House of them all. The twelfth home can be found directly behind the current one. This concealed House represents the hole in our karmic card. Whatever plants may be hiding here is a sign of significant karma. Concerns have been raised over the state of the planet. This House gives information on where or what kind of labour you may have done in previous life, such as where you may have incarnated. You would have been a participant in a significant number of revolutions if Uranus were there. In addition to that, you had Deja vu moments. Jupiter's placement in the twelfth House indicates a person has a "priestly" memory. When Pluto or the Sun is in the picture, you might recall times when you were significant. These prominent roles—king, emperor, and general—will be featured. Similar to Mars, Pluto is a name that conjures up images of battle. When a person fights in a war out of personal conviction as opposed to being forced to do so by the government, the karma that is accumulated is very different. This results in a load being placed on the soul. After the fall of Neptune, the soul may have already endured a significant amount of suffering to make up for the fact that it had previously evaded suffering.

CHIRON: It brings processes that occur below the level of consciousness or in the subconscious to the surface so that they might be healed. This is the planet of the wounded healer, suggesting where the soul must go to cure itself of the pain it has endured in its previous lives. Chiron in Aries, or first House, the ego, or self, is where the wound is located. Renunciation of the ego is likely required. Being at peace within oneself is essential to the healing process.

Healing any egoistic mindset can be accomplished by cultivating the awareness that "I am a soul." Chiron in

Taurus or Second House: The body, or the loss of one's sense of self-worth or security, is where the wound lies. Finding a sense of inner stability is necessary for healing. It is essential to unite the body and the soul.

Chiron in Gemini, or Third House: The pain comes from insisting that one is heard. It may make it difficult to breathe. Speaking one's truth is necessary for one's healing.

Chiron in Cancer or Fourth House: The injury is one of the emotions. The impact may be psychosomatic disease. Healing can occur when one emotionally detaches oneself from a situation as well as when one nourishes themselves.

Chiron in Leo or the Fifth House: The wound is in the heart or the way of expressing oneself. The road to recovery begins with removing authority and finding a solution to the head-heart conflict.

Chiron in Virgo or Sixth House: The wound may appear in your mind or your nervous system. Both striving for perfection and being overly critical of oneself can be harmful. Healing can be attained by being of service to other people.

Chiron in Libra or the Seventh House: The wound might be found in a person's relationship with others or with themselves. It is necessary to mend the rift between the demands of oneself and those of another and to locate an inner relationship.

Chiron in Scorpio or the Eight House: There is a possibility that the wound stems from a life-or-death situation or other traumatic event that has not been fully healed. Finding a way to acknowledge and make peace with one's shadow self is essential to the healing process.

Chiron in Sagittarius or the Ninth House: Long-held beliefs may have caused a wound in the soul, but attitudes can also be to blame for wounds. Reprogramming one's prior beliefs can bring about healing.

When Chiron is in Capricorn or the Tenth house: the skeleton may be carrying a wound from a past life and may show authoritarian traits. Finding one's inner authority is essential to the healing process.

Chiron in Aquarius or the Eleventh House: This person's spirit could be an alienated outsider who is blamed for the problems of the world. Finding common ground between the requirements of the individual and society is the first step toward healing.

Chiron in Pisces, or Twelfth House: The injury is a rupture in the relationship with the divine. The path to healing begins with an individual's realization that they are holy and their subsequent incorporation of this understanding into their daily lives. Not every illness we suffer from has its roots in the catastrophes of our past lives.

Sometimes, the offenders are the conditions of one's life, or they can even be sowing the seeds of a past existence.

Furthermore, the strains of the competitive and too-materialistic world we live in today compound the already heavy burden that our mental illnesses bear.

We are prone to feeling a great deal of sadness and anxiety because we are so easily sidetracked and overwhelmed by the routines of everyday life. The challenges of juggling relationships, employment, and social interactions occupy every moment of our lives. We need to attend to our daily necessities.

We forget that we are souls living in human bodies, which makes us vulnerable to emotional turmoil. It is our duty as souls to think and act with the highest kind and intensity of consciousness.

Since this is our ultimate destiny and our nature, spiritual beings must think and act like other spiritual beings. But when we allow the demands and rituals of everyday life to divert us and make us forget who we are, then sorrow, anxiety, and dread enter our lives. When this occurs, calmness, contentment, and inner delight are released.

The solution to this is also the same: By remembering who we are, we can allow the universal energy to pass through us and restore all the energy that past and present lives have blocked. The healing process can be strengthened by combining it with other techniques, such as childhood trauma recovery, past-life regressions, and others.

AFFIRMATION

: I grant myself forgiveness for self-blame.

: My karmic patterns are cleared, and I walk in the light of awareness.

: I am enveloped in eternal safety and security. I am a fulfilled soul in every conceivable way.

: I thank the universe for making me aware of the root of all my problems.

: From now on, I will only create positive and blissful relationships with myself, which in turn will build blissful relationships with everyone else around me.

: I allow my karmic body to be cleansed by all past negative energy of fear.

: I am free from the cycle of pain, which is keeping me stuck and moving toward the light.

Healing the Karmic Debt Expertise:

A Rollercoaster of Emotions—We must now put our baggage down to be permanently released from it, having realized that we are carrying it.

Now that we know the karmic pattern, it is critical to break free from it to have a positive outlook and live a complete life free from needless issues. While other methods exist to break out the karmic pattern, past-life regression is the most widely used. A person is transported to a previous existence through meditation, where they understand the cause of a particular event and ultimately find a solution.

This is a good alternative, but only a few people can afford it, and even those who can sometimes find it challenging to recognize the benefits and perform the meditation properly. This is merely a tiny sample.

There are other choices, such as forgiveness meditation, which is highly beneficial since it helps to remove the energy between two people by asking for forgiveness from the other person even when we do not know why.

Forgiveness is the finest approach to clearing a karmic pattern between two people or a group. The forgiveness meditation is helpful in situations like these, where you have not done anything wrong. Still, someone seems to despise you anyway, or when someone finds a method to make you feel horrible, you are powerless to stop them. This also functions in circumstances over which we have little control, such as when we are stuck and need help resolving a problem.

Even after you have exhausted all options, everything is still the same. You feel as though, no matter how hard you strive, money is just not able to enter your life. This could put you in a tight financial situation. Even though you may have tried every tactic under the sun, your financial circumstances might not have altered.

These practices—such as journaling, visualization, the law of attraction, and shift meditation—are beneficial and effective at helping us live abundant lives by rewiring our brains for success.

I highly recommend sticking with these practices, but incorporating karma cleanse is like adding salt to food. Karma purification will only speed up and simplify our lives by bringing about manifestation.

Therefore, adding it is advised to maximize our lives. You have no idea how amazing things may become when we begin to relinquish a weight we have carried for countless lives!

Take this as an example.

A doctor was diagnosed with cancer that refused to go away no matter what he did. He sought some doctors for assistance, and they performed a past-life regression on him. They discovered that he was a king in a previous life and had a fight with someone. He immediately drew his sword and killed the individual. He recognized it was confirmed when he was told. He asked him to forgive him with all his heart, and after a few months, he began to heal. He was utterly recovered after six months.

True, we don't always have access to former incarnations, and sometimes, we can't rest because our thoughts are playing tricks on us. In some situations, however, we do have access to prior lives.

There, we can offer "I'm sorry to whoever I have hurt in the past" along with our request for forgiveness.

We have to recite this line for at least ten minutes every day. Start at five minutes if you need more time. Regardless of the time of day, ask for forgiveness from the person as if they were before you. We are recognizing that energy is what makes each of us. These days, anything can happen. Therefore, we should be able to forgive someone for at least an hour every day.

Besides, we want to get into the hereafter with as little baggage as possible. Everything happens all at once. Therefore, we should keep our past devoid of karma to mitigate the severity of the issue. Even while we are helpless to change the way someone else behaves toward us, only they are capable of doing so.

However, we may still use meditation to send them good energy. If someone is bothering you and treating you poorly for no apparent reason, this strategy might be helpful.

Imagine if we cannot resolve the random morning trouble you receive from your boss. You have to get up each morning before them. You should wake up between 3 and 4 AM, which is a very fortunate and productive time to do anything if you do not know when you wake up. At that hour, most people are asleep, so the energy surrounding them is peaceful, sound, and pure.

Say things contrary to what they now hear to the individual you wish to heal. Let us say you're upset with your boss.

Send them positive energy as you think of them, such as

"You are such a pure soul,"

"You are a calm soul,"

"Your nature is to be calm and positive,"

 "You are an understanding soul."

Their subconscious mind is significantly impacted by our morning energy transmission, which gives them peaceful energy from us. There's a strong likelihood that if we're sending them happy energy, they will be doing the same for us.

They will not even understand why they feel good about us because it is our joyful energy that makes them feel good.

KEY POINTS-

1. Leaving Karmic Patterns Behind: The literature places a strong emphasis on the necessity of escaping karmic tendencies in order to have a happier and more satisfying life. This is discussed through a variety of techniques, such as forgiveness meditation and past-life regression.

2. The Abundance of Pardon: Even in cases when there has been no wrongdoing, forgiveness meditation is emphasized as a potent technique for releasing karmic patterns between individuals or organizations. Seeking forgiveness is said to help clear the air of bad energy and tensions.

3. Manifestation and Karma Cleansing: The book makes the case that rewiring the brain for success and prosperity may be accomplished using techniques like journaling, visualization, the law of attraction, and shift meditation. It is advised to combine these activities with a "karma cleanse" to accelerate the emergence of favourable results.

4. Sample Case: An actual case study of a physician's recovery via past-life regression and forgiveness is offered to highlight the possible

positive effects of clearing karmic difficulties on one's physical and mental health.

5. Transmitting Good Vibes: The book promotes the use of meditation to channel positive energy, especially when someone is mistreating you for no apparent reason. You might positively affect someone else's subconscious mind and receive the same in return if you offer them positive energy.

Relationship: Soul connection between two people

Physical characteristics never define a relationship. The reason we are talking about this subject is that most people struggle in this particular area of their lives. In the past, relationships were based on trust, contentment, and happiness. But these days, fear, rivalry, and jealousy rule everything.

Every connection has a term that describes it physically, such as "spouse," "parent," "child," etc., but what is a relationship between two people?

A link is established between two souls. A common misconception is that relationships are about "getting" and that our ability to "get" determines their strength. When we do not get what we want, it could be respect, love, or care; we tend to hold them responsible for our unhappy feelings, which we generated when we didn't obtain what we wanted from them.

That is one of the primary causes of the current state of unhappiness in our relationship. There are moments when we may ask ourselves why a relationship's foundation is still weak after a significant investment. Even when we appear to be doing everything we can, the other person does not seem to be content. It's likely because we pay little attention to the inside and are overly preoccupied with the outside.

Even if we try our hardest right now, we are secretly skeptical and critical of them. Thus, although everything seems ideal from the outside, the relationship is fragile.

Even though they appear to be kind and treat us well, there are moments when we feel uneasy around them and don't want to spend time with them. Conversely, we may come with someone with whom we bond deeply even though you don't do anything for them—you may only talk to them or offer minimal assistance. A deep sense of fulfilment and trust. This is because we were receiving energy other than just words.

Here, it is necessary to focus on transitioning from desire to giving. This implies changing this sentence to "I care for you," "I respect you," etc., instead of requesting that you respect or care for me. Any relationship in our lives—with friends, family, kids, spouses, etc.—could be the subject of it. Relationship problems frequently arise when we think we should receive in a relationship, but it's all about giving and giving. In these situations, we express our frustration by saying, "I am not getting what I want." Since we are the first to receive anything that we give, we are the first to experience anger before we vent it on someone else, for example, likewise with any other emotion.

Realizing that whenever someone says something to us, it is not because they think that about us; rather, it is just a reflection of their mental state at that particular moment. Even though we could have done a lot for them and they are still unsatisfied, it does not necessarily mean that we are the problem; instead, the other person is experiencing internal issues, which is when they most need our unconditional love. It is crucial to realize this since anyone might say something to us, and we may assume it has something to do with ourselves and develop hatred towards the other person.

Think back to all the individuals in your life and consider the experiences they may have had in this life and previous lifetimes that may have led to their behaviour. Choose to forgive them and show them compassion. It is pretty simple to forgive someone once we recognize that they are experiencing trauma and pain because we can understand why they are acting a specific way and don't take it personally.

We are being reached by the other person's energy and vibrations. The caliber of the thoughts they send our way determines the caliber of the vibrations. Building a strong, long-lasting relationship within our minds is crucial before attempting to construct one externally.

We often pay more attention to the outside world than the quality of our thoughts. Our brains have been imbued with manners since childhood. We were taught how to act appropriately and speak politely, which are admirable traits we should keep up with. The issue was that the focus was primarily on the outside rather than the inside.

We could not get into the habit of only thinking good things about other people to make friends. To build a beautiful and healthy connection, you need to be able to think of things. We might think that only we can see or hear our thoughts, so we don't pay much attention to them, which is untrue. Thoughts always come before words or actions. If someone thinks badly about us without us making those thoughts, they will affect us because our thoughts are energy. It also works the other way around: if someone likes us and we are not changing our thoughts, then their views will also make us feel good. How we think about that other person will change, for better or worse.

We will naturally begin to think positively about them if they are thinking positively about us and negatively if they are thinking negatively about us.

Therefore, if we think negatively about someone, say so to your manager, converse politely, and try your best to help them outside. These days, the relationship might be shaken by a slight fear or incident. All as a result of the ideas we had generated for them.

Moving forward, let us turn our attention inward and think loving and happy thoughts for all our loved ones, including strangers we encounter on the street. All of this helps to provide a solid basis for our partnership.

Key Points:

Caring Connections: Real partnerships are soul-to-soul exchanges that go beyond labels. Instead of external roles, they are based on enjoyment, fulfillment, and trust.

From "Getting" to Giving: It is essential to change from a "getting" to a giving and understanding mindset. Misplaced blame and unfulfilled expectations are common causes of unhappiness.

Comparing Inner and Outer Focus: Internal and external factors are balanced in a strong partnership. Things can appear flawless. On the outside, but interior negativity can weaken them. A relationship's base originates in the mind.

The Influence of Ideas: Our ideas have great power and influence the energy we release. Our connections are improved when we think well of other people.

Introspection and Optimism: Acknowledge that our ideas influence our words and deeds. We establish a strong foundation for happy relationships by purposefully thinking well of everyone.

Self
Determination

We frequently tend to blame people for our happiness or anger. Usually, our response is determined by what someone else does to us. It feels like other people bear the burden of our happiness or grief. We have allowed others to have remote control over our minds. When someone makes us feel good on an emotional level, they win our affection, and when they make us feel bad, they lose it.

We have been educated since we were tiny children that other people's actions affect how we will react. No one ever really took the time to tell us the truth because all they had ever known and believed in their entire lives was the same.

It's time for us to acknowledge that we must make the required changes. We rely so heavily on the thoughts, feelings, and actions of others toward us that the acceptance and gratitude of others dictate most of our daily actions.

Everything ought to depend on how the other person feels about it. To the point that, in an attempt to impress others, we even present a false image of ourselves that is entirely unlike the real us.

We may behave extremely extrovertedly toward those outside of us, do things we do not want to do, and drink things we don't want to drink even though we know they are unhealthy for us, but

we take these actions and destroy ourselves to appease others. This is but one example of the reality that many individuals in this globe are currently facing.

On the other hand, we may be entirely different at home, regretting our actions in response to peer pressure and understanding that what the other person says has nothing to do with us and everything to do with them is the first step towards mending.

We must remember this for ourselves, but we have a lot of terrible memories stored away in our minds since we were unaware of it.

Many individuals tend to assume that any statement or action made by another person is somehow intimately linked to them when, in reality, it frequently stems from the speaker's own personal struggles and past life experiences. Our outlook on the world and how we perceive others are heavily influenced by the circumstances we've encountered throughout our current lifetime and even in previous incarnations.

It is crucial to comprehend that our words and deeds may not always be met with enthusiasm by those around us, and that's entirely acceptable.

Each person possesses the liberty to interpret people and situations differently, and whether these interpretations have a significant impact on us depends on our own discretion.

A profound realization lies in recognizing that when someone communicates, they are primarily expressing their own thoughts, emotions, and past encounters rather than making direct judgments or evaluations about us.

Embracing this perspective can significantly enhance our capacity to navigate interpersonal relationships with a more profound sense of empathy and understanding.

KEY POINTS-

1.Dependence on Other People for Your Sense of Worth and Validation- Our emotional state is frequently based on the activities and behaviours of those around us. As a result, we allow others to dictate our enjoyment or rage based on their acceptance or rejection of us.

2.Acquired Worldviews- We learn early on that the way we respond to the acts of others depends on how they behave. It is important to remember, however, that this preconception is the product of one's upbringing and not an objective reality.

3.People-pleasing and deceiving oneself - Due to social pressure, we may act in ways that go against our values and ultimately endanger our health just to fit in. We may conduct ourselves differently in public than we do when we're by ourselves because of our desire to please other people.

4.Grasping the Root- Accepting that what other people say and do is more of a mirror of their thoughts, emotions, and experiences than a direct judgment of us is the first step toward self-improvement. Once we realize this, we may stop feeling like we need to constantly seek approval from others and start making decisions based on how we think.

SELF RESPONSIBILITY

We are cautious in communicating with others because we do not want to hurt them. We pay attention to even the most minor things, considering their requirements and preferences in everything from our attire to the gifts we give them.

The critical point to remember is that we speak to ourselves far more often than we do to other people, and most of the time, the things we say to ourselves are very different from the things we say to other people.

While we work hard to ensure the happiness and contentment of others, we could also undermine and hate ourselves because we believe we are undeserving of good things. This is a dangerous kind of energy we could give ourselves, and sadly, it is precisely the kind of energy we send to ourselves most of the time.

We should be cautious when we talk to ourselves in our brains because we should be mindful that we are always listening to ourselves, regardless of what we think, feel, or do. When you communicate negatively with someone else, such as when you say, "I don't like your dress," they might choose to accept or reject the message you're sending them. But in any scenario, we will be impacted by it since, despite their potential ability to reject it, we cannot do so.

Every idea we have influences our mental state, which in turn affects our feelings, which influence our behaviour, which ultimately determines our fate. We have to take back cognitive authority because of the way we think to effect the required change. It starts with self-perception, as our perception of ourselves shapes our perception of others. The initial phase in this process is accepting that we have a choice over our ideas and feelings.

Take charge of your thoughts and resist the urge to become their slave. You will always be a prisoner to your anger if you let it control you over anything that someone else has done to you. It would help to consider why you are allowing yourself to feel this way.

Indeed, creation is necessary because so many things and feelings seem to materialize out of thin air. As we are the ones who give birth to all feelings and thoughts, we also possess the ability to change them. Even while it's probable that things won't always go our way, our thoughts still have a responsibility to uphold. Recognize that you are the source of these unpleasant feelings and that, despite the situation, you can change, even if you are depressed or angry.

You'll only wear yourselves out more if you keep blaming other people and the environment.

Accepting the people and circumstances around you is the first step toward freedom. If I put the blame elsewhere for the situation, I would want the other person to change since I felt they were the cause of my suffering, but when my attention turned inward, the realization happened that I was the one who had caused the bad feeling. That's when the responsibility-laying ends, and I'm no longer under any pressure to change anyone's behaviour.

In this endeavour, cultivating a positive relationship with oneself must come first. Start recording your friends' and your thoughts regularly by writing them down. You may change a trend once you start to notice it. Through reiterating the idea consistent with the person, you want to be.

Positive changes in interpersonal connections will result from this over time. You'll start to see the two of you have a more favourable relationship.

Key Points

1. Self-Talk Matters: How we communicate with ourselves in our internal dialogue profoundly impacts our mental state, emotions, behaviour, and, ultimately, our destiny.

2. Positive Self-Perception: The first step in changing this internal dialogue is recognizing that we have control over our thoughts and emotions. We must take responsibility for our feelings and understand that we are the source of pleasant and unpleasant emotions.

3. Acceptance and Responsibility: Instead of blaming external factors, people, or circumstances for our feelings, we must accept our role in creating those emotions. Taking responsibility for our own reactions is essential for personal growth and freedom.

4. Change Starts Within: Cultivating a positive relationship with ourselves is the foundation for improving our interactions with others. This process begins with self-awareness, understanding our thought

patterns, and acknowledging our power to change them.

5. Mindfulness and Self-Reflection: Regularly reflecting on our thoughts and feelings and recording them can help us identify negative self-talk patterns. This awareness enables us to challenge and replace these negative thoughts with more positive and constructive ones.

Honouring our decisions

The most important thing is to make decisions that improve our inner strength and are only based on our values and goals. It's important to realize that other people's well-meaning advice often comes from their unique characters and points of view. Things that are easy for them won't always work for us.

People can feel guilty for a long time if they make choices with the help of outside factors and then hate them forever. The people whose advice we followed may also feel more connected to us in a karmic way, which could hurt the balance of our relationships. There are effects of every choice we make in life, both now and in the future. In every part of our lives, we have the power to choose.

Every day, our lives are whole of a constant stream of decisions, and in the end, these decisions have a cascading impact that determines our course. However, we frequently discover that others impact our decisions when we set foot on this planet.

As kids, we look to our parents, caregivers, and significant adults for direction and guidance. This relationship can become firmly engrained over time, making us seek the advice and opinions of close family members. People often find that they no longer have as much control over their lives as they used to as they get older.

We could make it a habit to ask other people for their thoughts and views, as we can learn from their unique experiences and points of view. Their wisdom might be perfect for them, but we need something else because our situation is different. We might give up our freedom without meaning to if we give in to other people's pull.

Things could go badly from here, mainly if the results differ from what we hoped. When something terrible happens because of a choice affected by outside forces, it is natural to look for someone to blame. Blaming someone else all the time can hurt our relationships and karma ties for the rest of our lives. This shows how important it is to be able to make decisions that are in line with our own values and goals and to take responsibility for the outcomes.

We live our lives because of them. To make choices that are in line with our beliefs and goals, we are the ones who are responsible for the big picture of our lives. Asking for feedback and help from people around us can give us helpful information and new ideas, but we should always make our own decisions. It is essential to think carefully about what might happen, weigh the possible outcomes, and listen to what others say. But the final choice should come from our own inner knowledge and gut feelings.

When you have to make an extensive choice in your life, this idea becomes even clearer. Take the choice to go down a specific job path as an example. People often get good help from family members or mentors who may point them toward a path that fits their experiences and values.

Even though this advice may be given with reasonable goals, the person must consider it. What gives them happiness? What gets them excited and fits with their unique hobbies and strengths? However, people can only find true happiness and success when they make their own decisions and choose a job that includes their inner calling, even if the advice and feedback they receive are helpful.

Asking for help and feedback from others while still having the final say on our choices should be a healthy part of making decisions. Giving your decisions to outside views can make you lose your independence and be blamed.

So, the important thing is to make choices that align with our inner knowledge and values. This way, we can be sure that our choices are accurate and give us power.

KEY POINTS-

1. Their biases and experiences typically colour personal Viewpoint-Advice from well-intentioned people, so it's important to remember that. Because our circumstances and objectives may differ, what helps them may not help us.

2. Regret and Guilt- If you let other influences sway your decision-making, you may regret your actions deeply. We experience inner conflict and discontent when we allow others to drive our decisions when those choices don't align with our ideals.

3. Karmic Connections-Taking: Taking the advice of others might upset the karmic equilibrium of our ties. We should consider how our actions will affect our relationships with people we look to for guidance.

4. Cascading Effects- No matter how seemingly little a choice may seem, it will have repercussions for us in the here and now and into the future. Knowing this, we may work to ensure that our decisions continue to reflect our individual beliefs, priorities, and experiences.

Shreyasi Shukla

Unconditional Compassion

A beautiful line that goes- "Perfect maturity is when a person hurts you, and you understand their situation, and you don't hurt them back."

When someone does something, it makes us question whether we can trust them or whether they were the way we thought they would be. At that point, our love is automatically stopped. When a child does something that their parents don't like, we start to question what they did instead of knowing.

The attitude we were supposed to give was love and acceptance for everyone, but we got the exact opposite. We sent more energy to refusal when the problem was more significant.

For some reason, we believe that our actions toward them are correct because of their problem. But the truth is that they were so weak at that point that it was our job as their friend and family members to accept them no matter what. Because they are in the most pain at that time—fear—we should not add to their pain. Instead, we should understand and show kindness. If we cause pain, we will feel more pain. Instead, the more love someone has, the bigger their problem will be, and love will heal it.

During a heated argument, one of our close friends can injure our feelings. The person who had been hurt responded not with anger but with compassion and empathy, showing that they understood their friend's troubles. Not only did their generous deed mend the rift in their friendship, but it also served as a powerful illustration of the transformative power of love that is not conditional.

This is just a little example, but when it comes to significant challenges in our lives, the love we feel should remain the same.

Because of this, we need to put this love into practice in the mundane aspects of our everyday lives, as this will undoubtedly be of assistance to us when we face more significant challenges. The real test of an individual's level of maturity is how they react when they have been wronged, and a mature person will show empathy and compassion rather than vengeance. Even when there are reasons to doubt one another, love should never waiver.

This guiding concept serves as a reminder to us that maintaining a consistent level of compassion is our most excellent source of power, whether we are dealing with everyday problems or serious challenges. We not only mend broken relationships but also better equip ourselves to deal with the vast challenges that life may throw at us if we cultivate love and empathy in our daily lives.

In the end, love is revealed to be the most potent force for change, able to heal even the most severe wounds and bridge even the most significant gaps between people. It is through this kind of unconditional love that we can discover our most authentic and committed selves.

KEY POINTS

1. Exceptional Wisdom and Kindness: When we are wronged by someone yet choose compassion over vengeance, we display the utmost level of maturity. Being able to look past the immediate behaviours of others and respond with compassion and understanding rather than anger or pain is a sign of emotional maturity.

2. Unconditional love: It's important to remember that love should ideally be unconditional, even when a person's behaviours cause us to question our faith. This involves keeping a compassionate attitude despite the other person's difficulties or harmful actions. In doing so, we aid their recovery rather than prolong their suffering.

3. The Transforming Power of Love:
The transformational power of unconditional love is seen in the narrative of a friend's compassionate response to an injury. The ability of love to heal broken relationships and propel development shines brightest in the face of adversity.

Shreyasi Shukla

Self-love

"The journey of our soul is made up of the choices we make, the experiences we have, and the lessons we learn in this life and during past lives."

These shared events have shaped and formed our personalities, affecting how we see and interact with the world. But in this complicated web of life, it's important to remember that our sense of self-worth is not tied to what other people think. Their likes or dislikes, acceptance, or disapproval, do not tell us what we are worth on their own.

Instead, our sense of self-worth comes from the safety of our minds.

This chapter is very similar to previous ones, as how we behave with others has much to do with how we behave with ourselves. In a world where people have very different points of view, no one has the power to tell us we are good or bad, worthy, or worthless. The decision on our character, the measure of how good we are, is something that only we can give. That shows how much we love ourselves and believe we are good enough just the way we are.

Because of this vital sense of self-love, we can ignore the criticism of others. Who we are and how we feel about ourselves are not susceptible to the ups and downs of other people's opinions. Our value is not dependent on their current desires; instead, it is a stable pillar of assurance that guides us through the waves of uncertainty.

We have been taught from an early age that we must rely on the approval of others to succeed in life, yet this is not the case.

It all started with the littlest details, like what to wear, and has expanded to encompass all aspects of our lives. This then depended on how we, in the present day, react when we encounter disapproval and rejection from another person and they say something that makes us feel unworthy, such as "you're useless" or "you're not good enough." We internalize this criticism as the truth about ourselves.

 One thing we must keep in mind is that everyone we encounter at that time will tell us their version of events. It reflects their character and the values they have developed over many lifetimes.

Imagine if someone you know died in a flood in a previous life, and now you are terrified of water, even though your parents have been asking you why you're frightened of water since you were a kid. Parents begin to doubt his fears and make the youngster feel something is wrong with him when all the child wants is love and understanding.

 Think about all the souls that have lived and died since then, each experiencing something horrible that has left them afraid even today. We assume they are doubting us because of something we have done, but it is more likely that they have been carrying this fear, or doubt, for a very long time; perhaps they were betrayed deeply in a past life, and it left an imprint on their subconscious so strong that they're still wary of trusting others.

We have to be there for them when they have no reason to distrust us but are yet carrying the energy of dread in their being, and we have to love them without question. Most people walk away, but if we can assist, we should not abandon the person.

On the other hand, there are times when we have to walk away from someone, such as when we are being physically harmed. Still, you should not hold it against them; instead, you should keep sending them positive affirmations like

"You are a powerful soul."

"You are a peaceful soul."

It is important to avoid thinking negatively about them, as doing so will cement negative karma between you.

Because we will send them negative energy, but if we choose to create positive thoughts towards them, the karmic energy from us will be of positivity only. Now think of all those people from whom we have some trouble, whom we believe are not according to us, and then just for a second, see them as a soul who has been on a journey for many lifetimes.

They are not role-playing like parents, friends' children, etc, but a soul. Their behaviors may not be how we want them to be, but I, as a soul whose fundamental nature is love, power, and compassion, choose to send them that energy only.

 Because they need it when they are at their worst.

Try this exercise before you go to bed or after waking up, and bring all those people you are having a problem with and see them as a soul and not the role they are playing in your life and not the body, just as a pure divine white light energy being.

 And now say that I understand why you are acting this way. I need nothing from you, be it emotionally or physically, and I will send you only energy of power, compassion, and unconditional and unadulterated love from now on.

Do this for a week and see how you won't be irritated by people as much as you would in the past. Instead, when someone is acting negatively, you will be able to understand them and not question their way of working and behaving from now on.

Now that we have an understanding of another person's behaviour and how they are behaving, it becomes pretty easy for us to disregard what other people are saying about us. Ever since we were little, our parents may have called us names such as obese, not intelligent enough, or not good enough. They may also have told us that we were not good enough. Whenever something like this occurs, you should remind yourself that these people were correct but only from their perspective; we have no idea what they must be going through to say things like this.

When we are in a good mood, even if anything goes wrong, we strive to react in the best way possible. On the other hand, when our mood is not good, even the most minor thing seems to bother us. You can observe this for yourself.

 Now, when we were kids, we might have been perfectly grand, but our parents might not have been thinking the same for themselves. They had to have been dealing with their struggles.

We do not know how their parents and grandparents treated them and, most importantly, how they must have lived their past lives. So, looking at it compassionately, we choose to forgive them, for which they have nothing wrong but expressing their opinion, which we took as children, and we decide to let go of all the labels. And all the other labels other people might have put on us, which we every day are fighting to prove them wrong.

Even if we become successful, what is the point of living for others? When it has nothing to do with them. Always and always and only we can define who we are, and no one else on this planet can do that to us. Because only we know ourselves better than anyone else in this world.

That is why to start with this mindset, stop taking appreciation; when we stop taking it and realize that what they are saying has something to do with us, we won't be able to stop taking criticism from someone else.

Start to give that love you want from others because, in reality, getting love from others is just an illusion. If someone loves us, they are reflecting their choices and personality, which has nothing to do with us; same with hate; if someone is jealous of us or hates us even when we seem to do the best, it is because they are reflecting their choices and personality which again has nothing to do with us.

Once we start to live with this mindset, then be it anyone, no one can harm us, cheat us, or reject us because no one has the power to do that.

 Then loving ourselves becomes the easiest thing in love because we realize we are already made up of love, which we seek outside.

This is what unconditional love means: loving ourselves and others without any conditions.

KEY POINTS-

1. Inner Worthiness: Instead of basing our feeling of value on what other people think of us, we should go inward. We should not measure our value by the approval or disapproval of others. Developing a healthy self-esteem in the privacy of one's thoughts is crucial. The Power of Loving Oneself Loving and trusting oneself makes one more resistant to the unkind words of others. Being secure in our values makes us more resilient to the ups and downs of other people's opinions.

2. Moving Away from Validation from Outside Sources: To be successful, we are taught by society to look to others for recognition and affirmation. Minor decisions, like what to wear, are the first step in a process that can affect every part of our lives. A person's sense of self-worth and self-love can be seen in how they handle criticism and rejection.

3. Taking others' criticisms to heart can be harmful: it is essential to work on developing an autonomous sense of self-worth. Going beyond the Understanding More Than Our Parts When we stop seeing people as their roles and start seeing them as souls on a journey, we get a glimpse of their true selves. This point of view allows us to ignore their actions and connect with who they are.

4. Feelings of Compassion and Love: It takes a lot of empathy and kindness to transmit positive energy of love, power, and compassion to others, especially when they may be hurting or at their worst. It's the idea that everyone deserves to be treated with compassion and acceptance no matter what they've done wrong.

CHAPTER 3

Embracing Change

The most valuable gift humanity has to offer is the ability to Think about who we are and then decide how to communicate it. We are blessed with this power every single instant.

Our experience gives us the chance to take advantage of this ability.

by our words and deeds, so stating and defining, for that instant, our identity within the cosmos.

From the minute you were born, you have been communicating who you are. were brought forth. During infancy, your subconscious means of survival and responses, such as eating, resting, and growing your motor skills, make you unique. When you were younger, you identified with how you pushed the boundaries and enveloped yourself globe. Your identity during adolescence was probably formed by the expression decisions you made when figuring out how to blend in and discover a space of acceptance in your culture and family and with your colleagues. When you were a young adult, your concept of self

The answers to your most profound inquiries are available at every turn in your life. In fact, from the moment you ask a question, it is as though they are waiting for you to let them into your life. Ironically, these responses frequently manifest most overtly in the individuals, locations, and events that are most resisted or avoided. It is the universe's most straightforward reaction to whatever you want.

No one's inquiry is unanswered by the cosmos; instead, it never stops offering fresh perspectives and encouragement on your never-ending path of consciousness expansion. Know that by rejecting the messages that life presents to you daily, you are depriving yourself of the answers to any questions you may have in life.

Any component of reality that you fight is a reflection of a part of yourself that you resist. How you relate to and identify with everything outside of yourself depends on who you believe yourself to be. Until you accept how this new perspective will transform You, you will not and cannot get anything in your external reality.

What you embrace and allow depends on how you view yourself. It also determines what you reject and what you resist.

Imagine yourself driving along an interstate highway, going about your business, when suddenly, the man behind the wheel of the car behind you begins cursing, swinging his fist, and blowing his horn at you constantly. It is a sign that you are unwilling to identify with the motorist if you cannot comprehend or tolerate this angry driver's actions. You must be compassionate with yourself before being sympathetic toward the driver.

You have to have enough self-assurance to recognize that the reason the driver behind you is angry doesn't have anything to do with you unless you were driving irresponsibly on purpose. You have made the angry driver's actions personal to you by believing they are directed at you, which is why you are offended by his rage.

You must acknowledge that you cannot determine the driver's reasons for irritation if you hope to remain calm. You have no idea what he is going through right now in his life. This person's wrath is directed at you in this particular situation, and he is using you as a focal point to let out his bad emotions. The irate gestures made by the driver are just an effort to get his inner equilibrium back. You are not enabling yourself to reach that degree of understanding if you do not have empathy for the driver. All you do is try to maintain the impression that you're a safe driver. You show that you must guard your pride if you react to the driver's rage by getting defensive or outraged.

This situation is intriguing because, unless you were driving carelessly, it is not really about your driving. If you converse with an angry driver, then the angry driver has successfully drawn you into his dramatic situation. Reacting similarly validates the driver's notion of hatred, rivalry, and conflict.

By getting upset and adding more Vigor to his tale, you have allowed yourself to be duped into accepting his delusion and rage. You had posed a question at one point that could only be addressed by learning more about who you are and how you approach life, which is how you contributed to the incident and why a driver like this would enter your world. Though you might not realize it initially, the experience of an irritated driver behind you is a good starting point. Perhaps a week ago, the query was, "How can I feel more at peace? Whether you accept or reject what is happening will determine whether you can identify the solution. Engaging with the driver presents an opportunity to respond and establish your identity. Maybe in the past, you've always jumped at the chance to get into arguments with other people. This may be your chance to pick a new adventure, or it could be the ideal chance for you to carry on with the current one.

Interestingly, reality repeatedly repeats comparable events until you grow weary of them. You will redefine yourself and, consequently, the energy you project in the following situation when you are sufficiently tired of the drama of interacting with angry individuals. Your new description of yourself can be like this: "I AM someone who is neither affected by nor engages with irate people." You physically change your experience when you change how you respond to anything.

When something like this occurs, people are left wondering and asking, "What is the explanation for this?" or "Why am I experiencing this? are revealed in the person you develop as a result of these encounters. The way you choose to respond to life's experiences and how they shape who you are might reveal their actual meaning. When you can regulate your reaction to what you are faced with every day and choose a new course of action for yourself, things shift.

The purpose of reality is always to provide you with solutions. This is the material world's only function. Every moment is a chance to learn more about who you are, what makes you unique, and the imaginative things you can become. Things appear out of nowhere when you ask questions, even if you are unaware that they are directly related to your inquiries.

It is always up to you to determine what to do with what appears. Every instant presents you with free will, the infinite option to respond to your experiences in a way that declares and defines who you are for that instant.

Think about this instance. A man who is homeless is seated on the side of the road. He asks you for a dollar as you walk by. Your response might be any of the following, depending on your worldview:

• You keep moving forward, pretend he doesn't exist, and hide your fear by not looking at him.

• You feel frugal, believing you do not have enough cash to give him any, and you continue to go forward.

• You walk away feeling resentment and disgusted, wondering why he does not get hired like everyone else.

• You come to a stop and hand him Rs1.

The opposition to what "is" is the foundation of the first three answers.

You disagree with anything that has appeared in your reality and have formed an opinion about it. In all honesty, you have no idea what this man's background or mental health is like right now. All you are seeing here is how this man is upending the way you currently perceive the world by putting reality that you wish to avoid encountering.

If you alter who you are, the circumstances surrounding you will also change.

There are always options and answers available to you in your world. Any response you provide is only proper or wrong, depending on the person you want to be. Are you content with your current self-definition and upcoming experiences, or are you prepared to act and react differently? What manifests in your life is not an accident. You pay attention to every series of occurrences, and each one provides an opportunity to discover more about yourself and find the solution to a question.

You are not the victim of your environment. You are the victim of circumstance.

The universe answers your questions and affirmations. Every encounter you have is always of some benefit to you. This is your reality's essence of perfection. Rejecting a specific experience indicates that you are not yet ready to recognize or accept the lesson the experience is trying to teach you.

A new, enlarged awareness is produced by the solutions to the questions that desire gives rise to. A new consciousness gives rise to new options, which in turn gives rise to new behaviours, which result in new realities.

You can ask meaningful questions for years and, at the same time, keep the answers from coming to you. You can argue that you already know the solution or do not need it. But the truth will always come to light in your reality. Your situation and mental condition reveal the reality. It will take longer to get what you want if you fight against the knowledge you need. It is a myth that acquiring knowledge and understanding requires a certain amount of time. A response can arrive quickly or take years to reach your consciousness. You are responsible for determining the process's timeline. The universal precept, "Ask and you shall receive," requires two elements to be implemented. Firstly, your request must be made with genuine desire. Millions of people engage in this daily practice by contemplating the various aspects of their lives, prayer, and meditation.

Here, you need to be willing to accept, where a lot of people install a barrier for protection.

Resisting the path of self-discovery can be difficult due to various strong emotions. These emotions frequently act as roadblocks to finding solutions:

1. Fear of Identity Loss: Fear of losing your primary identity and the familiar way of life you've always known if you embrace fresh knowledge.

2. Self-Image Concerns: Concerns about the person you will become if you accept this information, as well as prospective adjustments in your self-image.

3. Remorse for Past views: Feelings of regret for holding views contradicting the wisdom and direction you have received from loved ones.

4. Defensiveness of Being "Right: The need to always be "right" might make it difficult to accept that you may need to change your perception of reality.

5. Uncomfortable Self-Reflection: Feeling uneasy about how this new insight reflects your previous actions and choices.

6. Frustration Over Delayed Recognition: Dissatisfaction at not recognizing the truth sooner, which could have saved you from unnecessary difficulties.

7. wrath Toward Misleading Guidance: Frustration and wrath directed at previous incorrect counsel and attitudes.

8. Regret for Past Behaviour: A shame about previous behaviours and decisions that no longer correspond with your growing viewpoint.

These emotions can be impediments to self-discovery and personal growth. Recognizing and dealing with these feelings is an essential step toward accepting change and maturing into a more accurate and self-aware version of yourself.

These kinds of emotions reveal the real character of unsolved questions. These excuses are meant to keep you where you are and restrict your ability to become more conscious. You get a greater understanding of your genuine nature and creative powers instead of losing a part of yourself when you accept an answer and let go of a prior truth.

Fortunately, the answers will consistently come in proportion to your questions, regardless of how often you ask them. The truth will keep coming to light, and the more profoundly and intensely you inquire, the more the truth finds its way to you via your experiences. This even includes things that seem impossible to be true. It's not that you find it hard to believe what is occurring; rather, it's that you find it difficult to comprehend why it's happening.

It is like attempting to grip a ball underwater when one resists the truth. Some compare it to the relatively effortless feeling of holding down a tennis ball. For some, it is like trying to hold down a basketball, which requires a lot of strength and stamina. The reality is like holding a gigantic beach ball underwater for most people. Their egos battle with rejected yet necessary facts all day long in

a fruitless attempt to block out the reality that is straining to become apparent to them. They feel destroyed at the end of the day as a result. They are exhausted, both physically and mentally, from fighting against the status quo. They cannot acknowledge the truth that their reality begs them to recognize because of fear.

This cycle of events persists until a point is reached when an individual is forced to confront the all-encompassing reality, at which point the "beach ball" bursts to the forefront of awareness, floating there conspicuously.

At last, the deception ends, and the person regains the energy they expended, shielding themselves from this reality. The only option left is acceptance, which brings about a profound sense of freedom.

Truth and solutions can enter your consciousness without your reality degenerating to destruction. But for some, the lesson only reaches them through bad situations. Unwanted experiences will persist until you eventually decide to change who you are. It is flawless beyond measure.

Here are a few ways your desires might impact your creative energy:

1. When You Prioritize Ideal Career: If your desire for the perfect job outweighs your propensity to accept the first opportunity that comes your way, you'll be pleased with your current career.

2. Putting Fulfilling Relationships First: When the want to be in a meaningful relationship overcomes the need to be in a relationship, you

will have more successful and rewarding relationships.

3. Prioritizing Self-Love Over External Validation: When your need for self-love and acceptance from the inside outweighs your need for external validation and approval, you will experience a profound sense of physical and emotional security.

4. Eager Acceptance of Change: When your drive for answers and personal improvement outweighs your opposition to change, you can transcend static conditions and embrace transformation.

Once this fundamental principle is understood, you should be able to see it more clearly. This is how the universe functions. You create the exact circumstances that allow you to feel needy if you think you are in need. This occurs due to your constant desire to live up to your self-perception. Being at ease with life happens when you.

Recognize your desires and learn to let go of the urge for them to come true. This is significant because it indicates an awareness that you are entire and perfect just the way you are.

You are self-sufficient when you perceive yourself as whole and complete right now. You are entirely content with how flawless your experience was.

You don't have any false beliefs about who you are, and you don't avoid or disregard responses. Your pure faith now powers your will to know, taking the place of dread.

At that point, the responses start to come to you in a way that exactly matches your inquiries. The cosmos will provide this opportunity for you precisely when you offer this experience to yourself by realizing, accepting, and appreciating your beauty right now. Your identity is constantly changing and evolving.

Before you go through the required, frequently difficult experiences that expose your ignorance, you cannot genuinely know what you need to learn. However, you might choose to follow the never-ending path of viewing life with a more receptive and loyal mind. Suffering, wars, natural catastrophes, crime, and disease are all necessary for us as individuals and as a society to experience, consider, make decisions, and change according to our own free choice and in our own time.

Most of the time, the solutions you're looking for are directly in front of you, much like the seemingly misplaced keys you can't feel in your hand. You refuse to look at the obvious because you believe you already know who you are without keys. Your capacity to embrace and love this transient truth about yourself, as well as your readiness to trust in it, are what will allow you to experience your answers. Real wisdom is found in the experience that leads to realizing the answer, not the solution.

You have to do things differently, including looking at the world and yourself, to see new answers to your questions. How can you expect information that you have not experienced yet to come to light in a way that you are already familiar with?

Thus far, what do you "believe" you know provided the solution you were looking for? If not, it could be time to consider a different range of options. If you accept anything in a way that does not undermine or alter your beliefs about life, you won't be able to experience an answer to a perceived issue.

Only when you are no longer afraid of the truth it holds can a solution emerge. Any resistance to any aspect of your experience is a sign that you do not yet recognize that you are the one who created it.

You will be ceding this authority to the rest of the cosmos to create your experience if you do not think you are the creator of it. You will eventually experience negative mental states as a result of being used and controlled to the precise extent that you permit it to happen—a negative disparity results in discord. Negative imbalance not only prevents you from being creative but also makes it harder for you to recognize opportunities. Subsequently, the burden of feeling confined or stopped and lacking answers generates anxiety and perplexity that obstructs the boundless possibilities before you.

A person is not thinking clearly in this mindset and instead fixates on the worst-case scenario. Trying to see through the ocean's water during a storm is an excellent way to describe the state of the mind in this situation. It is nearly complicated to see through the turbulence and debris that is kicked up as the waves collide with each other from every angle.

It is the same with a disorganized mind. Until the imbalance is corrected, there is a marked lack of clarity. After that, harmony resurfaces in the ocean of the mind as equilibrium is reestablished. Everything becomes clear, everything calms down, and the quiet, crystal-clear water allows for ideal visibility.

You can find any solution you want in life with a healthy mind. Developing this mindset requires refocusing your attention in alignment with the reality that everything is possible.

 You will become as blind as if you are in the middle of a storm if all you think about is what you dread. Thus, if you want to get your answers, you have to make a conscious effort to

Recognize the fact that everything that occurs to, through, and around you are happening for you.

The truth is in front of you; you can choose to comprehend it or to reject or erase it. Pressure can be stopped in two ways: momentarily or permanently. It's common to choose ignorance over the truth. In actuality, resistance to the truth increases with the dread it inspires in others or themselves. People ask, "How? " Inquiries daily." and "Cause? And simultaneously turn down the answers that are directly in front of them. Great leaders killed or imprisoned for spreading their message of truth are common in history. to face.

Many people struggle with facing the truth of their circumstances because they want to avoid experiencing emotions of regret, guilt, or humiliation. This fact will not become apparent until a person realizes that there is no such thing as "fault" and that every decision they ever made was thought to be ideal at the time it was made. In a similar vein, every decision you have ever taken in your life has been one you felt was vitally important to your survival and identity at that specific moment.

There is nothing you can avoid from the past if you are no longer shielding yourself from all of the would, could, and should'ers. Now, without taking anything negative from it that would make you feel less of a person, you will utilize your memory of an unwanted experience as a guide for what you do not want to experience again. You are capable; you did not do your best in the past.

Of whatever future you think you deserve. You will then be receptive to any responses when you adopt this mindset. It is at this point that you will indeed see clearly.

Once the paralyzing energy of shame, guilt, fear, and regret has been released, the only mental state left is LOVE, which gives you the freedom to choose your life. There are only answers when you are living your life from a loving perspective, and they appear to you in any manner possible. Books, newspapers, TV shows, movies, remarks from total strangers, tragedies, and victories you encounter, billboards, license plates, your family, friends' unprompted counsel, dreams, and your intuition and gut feeling will all be more commonplace places to find them.

When you reflect, you will see that each experience you had along the way had a purpose. Since there is no longer a fake identity to defend, there will not be any messages that you are scared to embrace. It will, at last, realize and accept your value and attractiveness as a self-creating entity. Once you recognize and embrace this fact, your suffering will ultimately end.

This is the time in life when everything shifts drastically. You are prepared to embrace your excellence because you are worn out from the misconceptions you have dragged around for so long and depleted from the strife they have brought.

At last, you are ready to embrace a fresh perspective on who you are in the world and to love and create who you are. You are now receptive to the ever-present presentation of life-altering information in your reality. Your inquiries have brought each of the many "signs" you'll see into your reality, including this book. It will all make clear the incredible grace and strength that you have at your disposal to assist your ongoing creative expression and your journey toward understanding and serenity.

It's all a coincidence.

Every item or person that is a part of reality is in an eternal state of coinciding with something else. The word "coincidence" can be seen as a combination of the words "coincide," which means "to occupy the same place in space or time," and "incident," which means "event, occasion, or happening." As a result, everything in your life fits into this definition, not just "special events."

Everything else at the same time, demonstrating the flawless alignment of intents. This is the universe's graceful essence. You start to feel more of life's blessings when you accept this idea. As your intuition grows more robust, you'll be able to make quicker decisions and have more understanding.

Being aware.

You can start living each day more as a state of "being" than as a result of your acceptance.

You are no longer trapped in the past, dwelling on a bad experience or imagining a terrifying future. All you are doing is existing in the boundless possibility of this moment. When you are in this state of mind, the solutions keep coming.

Nothing visible to you is not flawless, and everything exists for You.

Your love and acceptance of YOU are reflected in your willingness to recognize and embrace the truth in your life. You have nothing to fear or need in this condition of openness as long as you believe that you are loved and influential in the world, you are. When you let go of the need for acceptance from anybody but yourself, you experience a profound sense of liberty. When you accept the perfection of where you are in life's learning curve, self-love naturally arises.

If the necessary prerequisites are not satisfied, intentions cannot materialize. Learning the conditions required to experience your highest intent consistently is what your life is all about. One of the most prominent and influential prerequisites you can set in place to accomplish this is complete self-love.

There is only one route to grace and self-love. You'll discover a new level of calm and peace as you navigate life, which helps to elevate the love and light in everyone around you as you open to your never-ending river of answers. You will see the apparent path of transformation ahead of you as the method to achieve any desired life experience is revealed to you. Synchronicities and intuitive messages will become widespread.

Creating a new reality is the next step towards becoming the person you can be. Equipped with enhanced self-awareness, you possess an unprecedented liberty to proclaim a fresh version of yourself and broaden the scope of your potential for your place in the cosmos. Every decision you make is a new version of yourself.

This results from the universe's most potent creative proclamation: I AM (THE SOUL).

CHAPTER 4

Unmasking the Illusions

Your mental state at any given time is the only thing that matters to your life experience because it determines the quality of your life. Every human being on the earth frames their worldview to achieve a contented and balanced state of mind. Their worldview is based on their experiences in this and their past lives. That is the reason that it won't be the same for everyone. This is our consciousness' intention moment by moment.

When we experience sentiments of happiness and calm, we believe that everything in the world is as it should be, that everything is flawless, and that everything is right with the cosmos. But this feeling mainly stays for a short time with us, and we then return to our old state of being.

There is a sense of calm and ease that is often difficult to describe. Many religions and cultures have given numerous titles to this state of mind throughout history. The names enlightenment, samadhi, bliss, nirvana, the kingdom of heaven, and being at one with God have all been used as this state of mind has no desires of emotional, mental, or physical satisfaction from the outside. This state of mind depends not on the outside but only on the inside with our connection to the divine. Each word describes roughly the same state of being, frequently presented as the ultimate state of mind to achieve, as that is our higher self's normal state of being.

Individuals described as experiencing this experience historically bathe in a glow that appears to shine forth from their faces in a palpable brightness. They exude a soothing and serene aura that others may sense when they are in their presence. Because there is no conflict or disharmony in their thinking, their presence is relaxing, welcoming, and loving. This state of equilibrium enables them to provide deep wisdom and insight to those who seek it.

This same condition of being is available to you at any time. There may have been occasions when you felt it for a brief moment or an extended period. It is never far away, and you have the potential to enter it at any time since it is at the heart of who you are. The path you are on in life is continually leading you to this realization. It is your fate.

No matter how many people throughout history have attempted to describe this condition of being and provide the world with their understanding of how to achieve it, most people still find it challenging. Many people find themselves continually oscillating between the polarities of feeling good and feeling nervous, feeling optimistic about life at first and then gloomy and despairing about it. They are rarely able to achieve proper long-term balance. Shifting back and forth causes people to wonder how to maintain a steady feeling of serenity and happiness. This all occurs due to the heavy, unsettled energy we carry from our past lives, which is still present in our auric field.

If you want to have more calm moments, one of the first things you will be advised to consider is that there is no place to "get to" at "some time."

The irony is that the mental state you want is RIGHT NOW. It only takes your knowledge and acceptance of "what is" now—"what is" referring to what is known as the truth. This is the realization that everything in the present moment is perfect, including you. Accepting this reality is all required to set you free to enjoy this magnificent state. While calm and serenity are deeply ingrained human desires, the path to achieving them is fraught with misunderstanding and confusion.

Fortunately, unpleasant states of mind are caused by a misunderstanding of the nature of calm and satisfaction, both completely adjustable. Every soul can develop a tranquil and balanced state of mind by the simple intention and desire to do so. It is not denied to anyone as it is our normal state of being. Everyone who sincerely and intensely wishes for the experience can enter a condition of grace and calm.

To obtain the desired state of mind, you must first recognize certain essential truths regarding its formation. One of the first and most critical realizations is that you have always produced your mental state. You may not have realized it, but that doesn't make it any less accurate.

Your mind is created by your vision of who you are (I AM) in connection to your ability to experience this expressed vision (the confirmation or denial of the ego).

You are in one of three mental states at any given time.

You have been accepted:

1. You might unintentionally limit your fantastic potential and keep yourself in a lower-energy state by accepting the assumption that you are exclusively defined by the labels connected with your career, financial status, or gender.

2. A balanced mental state stems from the realization that the person you identify with, based on your labels, has succeeded by living up to the expectations of society surrounding that identity. Using sensory awareness, everything was finished.

3. A more or less positive state of mind resulting from the fact that who you feel yourself to be is not only being reinforced by your experiences and perceptions, but has grown into an even wider self-definition than you had previously considered conceivable.

Here is an easy example.

1. You've been diligently working on a personal project, pouring your heart and soul into it, and it's finally completed. You present it to your peers,

who respond with awe and admiration. This moment aligns perfectly with your self-perception as a talented and capable individual. Your state of mind is one of joy and pride. You might say, "I knew I could do it!" "I'm so proud of myself!" "This is a great accomplishment!" Your ego is basking in the glory of confirming your self-definition.

2. You've been training for a marathon, and the day of the race has arrived. As you cross the finish line, you realize that you not only completed the race but also achieved a personal best time. This moment reaffirms your belief in yourself as a dedicated and disciplined athlete. Your mental state is one of triumph and exhilaration. You could express your feelings with phrases like, "I did it!" "I'm on top of the world!" "This is a major achievement!" Your ego is revealing in the validation of your self-image.

3. You've been trying to learn a new language, and after months of hard work, you have a fluent conversation with a native speaker. This experience resonates perfectly with your self-concept as a determined and capable learner. Your emotional state is one of sheer joy and accomplishment. You might exclaim, "I can't believe I'm doing this!" "I'm so thrilled!" "This is incredible!" Your ego is basking in the satisfaction of reinforcing your self-definition.

These examples illustrate how our emotional states can be influenced by the alignment or misalignment of our actions and accomplishments with our self-perceived identities.

Each life experience allows you to accept or reject "what is." It is formed by the collision of who you define yourself to be and your experience. When your self-definition (I AM) is validated, you feel at peace with the cosmos. If it is not acknowledged, you will feel less alive and will be in a hostile and disharmonious condition. If your self-definition is not only validated but also grows in differentiation, you enter a pleasant, positive condition, feeling more alive than ever before.

Your desire to acquire a more bearable state of mind, together with your views about how to obtain that state of mind, will always be the driving force behind your decisions. That is why many people opt to seek addictions to improve their mental health. Take a tablet if you are feeling down or nervous. If you are feeling lonely, have a drink. If you are unsatisfied with your appearance or body, you can pay to alter them. If you do not feel appreciated, go out and buy something. These quick-fix shortcuts to a higher state of mind are only transitory (forming the addiction) and have the potential for negative consequences. Finally, the core reason for the perception of an unfulfilling existence has not been addressed. The cycle merely continues until your desire for a more serene state of mind leads you along an inner path of discoveries that helps you to begin to realize who you indeed are.

Many people are unaware that their self-defining affirmations of I AM have the potential to influence their reality. Because of this misperception, they tend to feel that their past experiences reflect who they are now and are inextricably linked to their identity.

The way we embrace external labels can be understood as follows:

Just as our soul can adopt and identify with various external labels, it reflects our journey of self-expression and growth. These labels become the facets of our earthly experience, similar to the examples shared previously:

1. "I AM a creative artist." - This person has always embraced their creative side explored various art forms, and it is a fundamental part of their identity.

2. "I AM a dedicated environmentalist." - This individual has consistently shown commitment to environmental causes, taking actions to reduce their ecological footprint and promote sustainability.

3. "I AM a passionate chef." - This person's love for cooking and culinary exploration is a defining aspect of their identity, and they have honed their skills over the years.

4. "I AM a loving parent." - This belief represents someone who has consistently shown love, care, and dedication to their children, making their role as a parent central to their self-identity.

5. "I AM an avid traveller." - This person identifies strongly with their passion for exploring new places and experiencing different cultures, making travel a core part of their identity.

6. "I AM a fitness enthusiast." - This individual's commitment to regular exercise, healthy living, and maintaining physical fitness is a defining characteristic of their self-image.

7. "I AM a lifelong learner." - This person has a continuous thirst for knowledge, always seeking opportunities to expand their understanding and skills.

These examples reflect positive and enduring self-identities that don't involve overcoming negative past experiences but instead focus on embracing and affirming aspects of one's identity that bring them fulfillment and joy.

These labels, if tightly defined, can limit the soul's potential. However, it is critical to note that they can also be helpful instruments for self-expression and progress during the soul's earthly journey. Rather than viewing these labels as defining the entire soul, we can understand them as descriptions of the job we do and the roles we play in this physical sphere.

We empower ourselves to transcend the constraints of these classifications by realizing that our identity extends beyond these labels and by keeping open to the endless possibilities of self-discovery and progress. This allows us to thoroughly explore the depths of our potential and align with our temporal path, eventually achieving the harmony and contentment mentioned in the previous example.

The transition to a supposed new self-declaration quickly produces a unique experience while leaving behind the undesirable identity and the energy that formed it in the past.

Who you were before is not who you are now. You decide who you are at any given time. Your previous self-definition will influence your present and future experiences to the extent you allow it. Your mental condition is everything. As you learn more about how this state of mind is generated, you can take conscious control and create it exactly how you want it.

Being in a powerful state of awareness where you perceive all things are possible leads to a tranquil place of contentment and serenity. Time pauses, and you are in complete harmony with the moment when you are in this state of balance that is devoid of any emotion. When you come to ultimate acceptance of where you are in life concerning everything else, you integrate into the moment. To be in this state of mind means to have complete comprehension and love for oneself, knowing and comprehending that, for this time, you are perfect, and everything around you is perfect.

To achieve this liberated state of mind, you must examine the dominating thoughts you have about yourself that prevent you from perceiving yourself and hindering your connection to the source.

These thoughts tell you that you should be more, and they are the source of your energy and mental state being out of balance and out of sync. Peace will not be realized until you acknowledge the source of the "disconnect" and embrace the truth and perfection that the moment has to give.

CHAPTER 5

LIVING IN PRESENT MOMENT

Calm down and take some nice, long, deep breaths because this moment, right here and right now, is precisely where you are meant to be. There is neither another location nor another time.

This is the end. This moment, just like every other one in your life, is crucial to you and serves a particular purpose. The perfection of what you are experiencing results from every question you have asked and every circumstance and share you have gone through and conquered to get to this moment and these words now.

This perfection has emerged as a result of all of these things. The gift of this moment, which will last forever, is whatever you choose to take away from it. What has been presented to you in various ways throughout these words is the emancipating self-awareness that how you create and experience each moment of your life is always within your control. Your willingness to love who you are in this very moment is the single most crucial factor in determining the quality of your life. This love brings you to a beautiful place where you can accept the world surrounding you.

It also leads you to the realization that you always have the power to choose the circumstances that determine what "will be" in your life. The journey of self-awareness you are currently on is the path of answers that dispel the disharmony associated with the questions that arise in your mind regarding who, what, why, and how. You are currently on this journey. The essence of your transformation into a person who is more at peace with yourself, more creative, and more fulfilled lies in increasing your awareness of who you are.

This fresh perspective on how to exist in the world arises from the realization that one must first acknowledge, love, and respect their existence. The only way to achieve actual change is for you to change first and foremost. Everything else is just a diversion that makes the passage of time feel longer than it is.

Because unconditional love is the most potent force in the universe, your thoughts that express love and acceptance for who you are right now — precisely as you are — are a highly significant component of your spiritual development. Love that is not conditional alleviates all forms of anguish, including fear, resistance, and separation, as well as any suffering associated with these conditions. The feeling of peace, harmony, and unity is all left after all of these illusions have been dispelled when you do this. When you love yourself completely, for the simple reason that you realize that any reason that prevents you from experiencing this kind of love is wholly erroneous, you make it possible for the most significant potential of who you are to come to life and shine its light.

This light and energy possess the potential to be of service to the entirety of the world. Unconditional love is the spirit and energy of serving all of life.

It is free from need, and it does not ask for anything in return. Your entire perception of life will shift once you reach this level of self-love and acceptance, though. When your mind matures to the point where you love yourself more, you are freed up to see an incredible variety of creative opportunities for your life that you were previously unaware even existed. A sense of gratitude for everything you are and everything you have experienced that has brought you to this point will accompany the new opportunities that present themselves to you as these possibilities unfold.

You have had a significant impact and purpose in the lives of others, just as everyone who has ever been a part of your life, whether briefly or permanently, has left a significant mark on you and contributed to who you are today. The critical message that the universe is trying to convey to you every day is that YOU MATTER, and it does so in the form of the YOU MATTER acronym.

Until this point, every thought, action, and reaction you've had has served a purpose not only in your life but also in the lives of everyone you've interacted with. This is true not only for yourself but also for everyone else. You can enter the only moment you will ever have, which is the one you are in right now, when you realize the truth about the perfection of your past and make peace with it.

The only place where you have the opportunity to tap into more of your unlimited power and create more of who you want to be and how you want to matter in the world is in the moment that you are currently living in. You are not who you believe you are, but you are always so much more than who you are. Who you were a month ago, a week ago, a day ago, or even just five minutes ago is not the same person as who you are right now. You are perpetually evolving due to expanding your consciousness due to the process of gaining experience, interpreting that experience, acting on what you've learned, and reacting to what you've learned.

Everything revealed to you while reading this book has been a component of this evolution. The following statements may reflect recent changes in your awareness that illustrate a new change in your capacity for self-love.

These changes may have occurred as a result of reading the following statements.

• You once experienced feelings of regret because you believed you should have performed more admirably in the past. You can now accept yourself because you realize that if you had been able to serve better, you would have.

• In the past, you harboured contempt for others because you believed they should have performed more admirably. You feel compassion for them now because you know that if they could have done better, they would have done better.

• In the past, you felt proud of yourself because you believed you were "better than" someone else. You are now humbler due to realizing there is no such thing as bettering or worsening oneself.

• You formerly experienced hatred because you fought against the presence of something or someone. You can share love now because you have realized that everything that happens to you serves a higher purpose that is always for you.

• In the past, you experienced shame because you believed you were unimportant. You now have honour due to realizing that you will always be necessary.

• In the past, you were subjected to chaos due to your resistance to change. You have finally realized peace because you have accepted that you are an existence that is constantly evolving.

• In the past, you experienced anxiety because you believed that other people would not love you. You have attained faith because you realize that the ultimate source of love resides within you. When these concepts become ingrained in who you are, then and only then will you experience peace. As soon as you realize and accept that your moment-to-moment perfection is a reality, you will begin to experience perfection.

Because your capacity for self-love and acceptance is always reflected in you in the experiences and energy of your life, you always know where you stand about this awareness. Your life is an ongoing journey of expanding your awareness of what is possible for you, which is what life is all about. Your awareness is increasing with each passing day, minute, and second. Your thoughts and beliefs will shift to accommodate the expansion of your awareness.

As you gain a deeper understanding of who you are and the boundless scope of what you are capable of knowing and producing, new opportunities will present themselves to you. The constant cultivation, acknowledgment, and expansion of one's possibilities are the driving forces behind inner calm and composure. You determine the pace at which you advance toward a more satisfying life.

You will have questions, and the answers to those questions will appear in all nooks and crannies of your reality because no experience that you have in your life is pointless. The answers to your questions will present themselves in a manner that is mathematically precise and directly proportional to the degree to which you yearn to have those experiences.

They are currently located in this very location. You are now on a path that will bring you a greater awareness of this fact, which is exciting!

You hold the key to unlocking the mysteries of the universe and steering the course of your unique journey through life. You are the only thing standing between yourself and a life of peace and harmony and a life full of fulfillment.

The path of intentionally creating life is comprised of a reiterative cycle that includes the following five steps:

1. Begin by questioning and desiring to understand your soul's purpose and potential.

2. Acknowledge that the answers you uncover resonate with the truth of your soul's essence.

3. Embrace the understanding that labels can serve as tools to express your soul's journey without becoming your core identity (I AM).

4. Infuse your newfound confidence and purpose into your actions, manifesting your soul's path with faith.

5. Experience the profound completeness of your soul's accomplishments along this transformative journey.

Love The universe will only react in a way that corresponds to the identity you genuinely believe you embody. If you need a perfect relationship with yourself, a better state of mind, and a much calmer life, then the universe will most certainly grant you that experience through the continued creation of need.

When you love yourself enough, and when you see your authentic, unlimited worth and perfection, you will no longer consider yourself to be lacking or incomplete in any way as you as a soul are always complete and connected to everything that was ever made and ever will be.

By realizing it, you also allow yourself to take the new actions necessary to make your dreams a reality.

You are never who you were or will be; what matters is who you decide to be right now.

You must act faithfully to demonstrate that you genuinely love and believe in yourself. This is what the universe reacts to on a fundamental level.

As you establish your belief in God and love for others, you become a source of inner fortitude and motivation for others to draw from in their moments of need as they face obstacles on the journey toward inner tranquillity and self-actualization.

Because your beliefs about who you are the key to what you create in your world, we have compiled a list of several powerful ideas for you to contemplate for your life and incorporate into your daily routine. Before this moment, if you had feelings of guilt, shame, or regret about certain events in your life, the weight of these thoughts may have caused you to suffer in several different ways.

You can choose to free yourself from the suffering by replacing those thoughts with the loving thought that follows:

"I know that everything that happens in my life is for my highest good only."

Even if there are something I have done in the past that I do not particularly approve of, I will use the knowledge and insight I've gained from those experiences to make better decisions right now. I will make different decisions because I have announced that I am not the person I used to be; instead, I am the energy, the creator of my every thought, word, and action. The burden of these thoughts may have caused you to feel angry, hurt, and physically drained. If you held judgment and contempt for people, you thought were responsible for the current conditions of your life, the burden of these thoughts may have caused you to keep these feelings.

Do not give in to the power that these thoughts have over you. Make the conscious decision to supplant them with the following thoughts:

"I accept complete responsibility for the choices I have made that have brought me to this point."

As the conscious director of my life, I have decided to reclaim this power of choice now, even if I have in the past given someone else control over my ability to choose. Everything that happens to me serves a purpose and is the consequence of my past thoughts and actions. At any given time, the universe is demonstrating to me precisely what it is that I need to understand and acknowledge to get exactly where it is that I have asked to go.

I have decided to accept everyone and everything that is a part of my experience and take 100% charge for it. From now on, I choose to shift my identity from being body-conscious to soul-conscious and reclaim my original identity of the self.

You may have been experiencing feelings of directionlessness, lostness, and being trapped in the current experience of your life if you have not believed that you are good enough or worthy enough to have the experiences that you dream about having. Stop allowing these beliefs to direct how you live your life.

Make the conscious decision to supplant them with the following thoughts:

"As a soul, I am the boundless creator of my reality, wielding the infinite power of the universe to shape my life according to my desires and beliefs. My existence is a canvas of endless possibilities waiting for me to paint it with the vibrant hues of my dreams and aspirations.

With unwavering self-belief and a deep connection to my inner essence, I embark on my life's journey, knowing that every challenge is an opportunity for transformation and growth. I am the author of my destiny, scripting a life filled with abundance, joy, and fulfilment.

I understand that the universe conspires in my favour, manifesting my desires as I align my thoughts and beliefs with the highest good. I am a magnet for positivity, attracting the people and circumstances that enhance my life and propel me toward my goals.

With each passing moment, I deepen my faith in the incredible power within me. I am the alchemist of my reality, turning challenges into stepping stones, fear into courage, and doubt into unwavering conviction.

My journey is a testament to the transformative influence of self-love and belief in my inner potential. I am a living testament to the magic that unfolds when I acknowledge the limitless power of my soul and trust in the extraordinary life I am creating."

This affirmation underscores the notion that, as a soul, you can shape and transform your life by harnessing the power of belief and self-love.

However, if you are unaware of your essence, you will act accordingly. You will eventually realize, as the journey that is your life continues to unfold, that at your very centre, you are complete just the way that you are. When you finally realize this, you will realize that the love you fought so hard to obtain from the outside world has always been within you because you are love. When you finally have this understanding, you will realize that.

At this level of being, rather than needing this love, you can give it freely, without conditions, and end. Love is the only thing that is in store for you. There is an elegant simplicity and beauty to life that can be found once one gets past the deceptive ideas of self-limitation and lack. The more you allow yourself to be open to seeing the beauty and simplicity that lies within you, the more fluid and peaceful your life will become. In this region of existence, time seems to dissolve into an endless moment, and there is a sense of connectivity and oneness with everything in the universe.

You have realized that to feel that any thought is natural, you must first become the creator of the thought and then embody it. For instance, many people think they require love and respect, and they go through their days trying to "get" those things from the outside world. They don't understand that you don't "get" love; instead, you become loving by showing love to yourself and others, and as a result, you realize you are already the energy of love and release the need to get it from outside.

You do not "get" respect; instead, you "become" respectful by respecting yourself and others, and as a result, you are already in an energy of respect that you thought could only be fulfilled if you get it from outside.

You don't "get" peace; instead, you become peaceful by contributing to the peace of the world around you, and you continue to be quiet as a result.

The great paradox of faith is that to demonstrate that you already possess what you want, you must first give up the "want" of it.

The creative assertions that follow are among the most potent that you are capable of making. You will know you are well on your way to living the life of your dreams when you accept and incorporate these truths daily into who you are as a sign that you are well on your way to living the life of your dreams.

• "My presence holds significance within me which radiates to the outer world.

• "Every moment in life, guided by intuition, carries a unique purpose for my journey."

• "Love, an essence of me, flows through me, surrounding and filling my being."

- "I, with the guidance of my intuition, shape the experiences in my life, defining who I am."

- "Through the lens of my wisdom, I exist." In the spirit of "I AM that I AM."

When you reach a level of self-acceptance and love that is so complete that you are indeed free of the opinions and ideas that other people have about who you are, other than your own, you will be able to experience true peace and contentment in your life. This will be the case when you have reached this state.

At this point, there is nothing that can have a detrimental impact on the way you are feeling mentally anymore.

Nothing that you experience will ever be evaluated or resisted in any way. When love reaches this level, there is no longer room for worry or anxiety. Even death itself is seen as nothing more than a stage in an endless cycle of the transformation of energy and matter that has been going on since the beginning of time and has no end.

As a result of attaining a new level of transcendent awareness and comprehension, you transform into a rock of love and peace. When you are at peace, you can see the truth, which is that the divine nature of everything that exists is guiding you toward expanding your awareness of oneness and love.

This expansion's forward momentum is the inertia of all the energy contained in matter. Your consciousness develops further and further with each passing moment. You originated from nothing to become something, and you will eventually go back to nothing to become something once more. Grow, then shrink, then grow, then shrink. Repeat. This is the rhythm that all life in the universe uses to keep time with itself.

Your experience of reality is a progression of consciousness that will, in the end, bring you to a conclusion that is both awesome and astonishing. Your own choices and decisions will always drive your life's journey at its core.

Now is the time to get out there and become more of who and what you already are. Put your newfound knowledge to use so that you can live a life that is rich and fulfilling. Always go with love by drawing on your knowledge of what is real and your connection to it.

Make use of everything to feel at ease as you consciously create a new version of yourself to be the fearless and trustworthy driver of the life of your dreams. You have never been without access to the answers that could have brought you some measure of serenity. This moment is your opportunity to put these realizations into action and experience a new version of yourself. You will experience more of the splendour of the limitless love source that is you as you claim the grace of awareness.

As you do this, you can see it more clearly. You will step out into the world with a whole new identity of the self with complete gratitude for unwavering faith in your mission and boundless love for how you express yourself. An incredible realization hits you as you comprehend and accept the potent idea that you are the creator of your reality, and it is at this point that you will find that you have arrived. When you finally realize that every moment of your experience is created by your beliefs and your will to confirm those beliefs through your life experience, it can be a very empowering realization.

It presents an entirely fresh angle from which to examine your life and the choices you have made, considering what is important to you and how those choices have impacted you along the way.

Everything in the universe, at every instant, creatively displays some aspect of its identity to convey that identity to other things. This identity manifests itself for you in the circumstances of your life as they are right now, as well as in how you interpret and respond to the various situations you find yourself in. Your resulting state of mind and the quality of your life are both products of this cycle, which consists of perception, reaction, and the degree to which each circumstance is made to "matter," which becomes every one of your life's experiences.

What you give attention to and what you perceive to be important in your life are the two factors determining what you experience as "matter" in your world—the matter before you only come to life due to your intention and attention. The only way for what you go through to have a discernible impact on you is to give it significance in some way. If you do not give it any importance, it will not have any influence on you.

Realizing our true selves, our oneness with the divine, and our own divinity is the essence of spirituality.

CONCLUSION

As we end our adventure through "Soul Consciousness: Realizing Our Divine Connection," we find ourselves at the threshold of a significant transformation. Each chapter of this book has been more than just words on paper; they have been portals into the depths of our minds. We have set out on a quest to learn more about ourselves, and now we're on the cusp of finally seeing the brilliant light that's always been there.

Our journey has been a spiritual and intellectual voyage that has opened our eyes to the infinite possibilities. As "Soul Consciousness" has shown us the importance of our thoughts and deeds, it has also given us the tools to use this awareness and agency for good.

Every time we make a deliberate decision, we have the chance to illuminate not only our path but the route forward for those around us by unleashing the powers of love, compassion, and development.

Understanding karma and rebirth has helped us unravel the ties of fate that bind our lives together. Looking back on our lives, we can see how every decision and action contributed to the bigger picture. We've uncovered the timeless character of our trip by tracing its connections through time. With this information, we may write the next chapter of our lives and develop into conscientious architects of our destinies.

It is a beacon of peace and meaning in a world that might feel dark and chaotic at times. It's a call to action to shine brightly despite the chaos around us, a reminder that our efforts not only dispel our darkness but also help others find their way. This trip has been an eye-opener, a reminder that each of us has the potential to bring about profoundly beneficial change in our own lives and the world at large.

As we approach the climax of this profound investigation, may it be a springboard for a renewed dedication to the awakening of our soul consciousness. The essence of our purpose and the secret to a life intimately connected to the divine can be discovered by embracing the light inside, making conscious decisions, recognizing the tapestry of our destiny, and being beacons of light.

This book, "Soul Consciousness," is more than a milestone in our lives; it's a declaration of our never-ending commitment to personal growth and spiritual development.

Soul Consciousness